volume V numbers 2 & 3

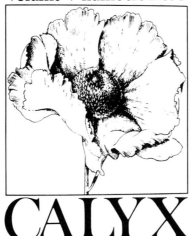

CALYX

GRATEFUL ACKNOWLEDGEMENT IS MADE TO THE FOLLOWING FOR PERMISSION TO REPRINT COPYRIGHTED MATE-
RIAL:

Casa de las Américas: "Estelli," By Claribel Alegría is from *Sobrevivo*. "The time that has passed…," by Gioconda Belli, is from *Line of Fire*. © 1979 by Casa de las Americas, XX, n. 117.

Dvir Co. Ltd.: "Tune to Jacob…" and "Rachel Cried…," from *Tree Reached to Tree*, © 1978 Dvir Co. Ltd., Mzaeh Street 58, Tel Aviv, Israel.

Editions Gallimard: "Les témoins," "Le Vide," and "Initiales," by Edith Boissonas, are from *Initiales*. © 1971 by Editions Gallimard.

Suhrkamp Verlag: "Someone is Silent" and "Always Something Else," by Elisabeth Borchers, are from *Gedichte*. © 1976 by Suhrkamp Verlag, Frankfurt am Main.

Fondo de Cultura Económica: "Commission," "Love," "Return," and "Kinsey Report," by Rosario Castellanos are from *Poesía no eres tú*. © 1972 by Fondo de Cultura Económica.

Aguilar Editorial: "Those that sing…," by Rosalía de Castro is from *Rosalía de Castro, Obras Completas,* © 1968 by Aguilar Editorial. "A tame river…," and "in their prison…," by Rosalía de Castro are from *Obras Completas de Rosalía de Castro,* Tomo I. © 1974 by Aguilar Editorial, Juan Bravo 38, Madrid, Spain.

Li Chi: "On Arriving at Ling-nan, January, 1949," by Li Chi is from *Li Chi shi tz'u chi* (Taipei: Yi Wen Publishing Company, 1975). © 1975 by Li Chi.

Classen Verlag: "Interview," and "My curiosity," by Marie Luise Kaschnitz, are from *Dein Schweigen, meine Stimme: Gedichte 1958-61*. © 1962 by Classen Verlag, GMBH, Düsseldorf.

Editeurs Grasset: "They invented the body…," by Anna de Noailles, from *L'honneur de souffir* published in 1927.

Suzanne Paradis: "Anguish," by Suzanne Paradis, is from *Pour les enfants des morts,* published by Editions Garneau in 1964. © 1964 by Suzanne Paradis.

Alejandro Storni: The poems "You Want Me White," "I'm Going to Sleep," and "Humility," by Alfonsina Storni, were originally published in *El dulce daño* (B.A. Sociedad Cooperativa. 1918) and *Ocre* (B.A., Agencia general de libreria y publicaciones, 1927) respectively. All rights belong to Alejandro Storni.

Hermann Luchterhand Verlag: *Paulinchen war allein zu Haus,* pp. 5-15, by Gabriele Wohman. © 1969 by Hermann Luchterhand Verlag.

Petra von Morstein: "Thing Poem," "In the Case of Lobsters," and "Present," by Petra von Morstein, are from *An Alle*. © 1969 by Petra von Morstein.

Every attempt has been made to determine copyright holders of all work included in this issue and to clear permissions. If any have been overlooked, the editors would appreciate being informed for future editions.

CALYX is available by subscription: one year (three issues) $10.00, two years $18.00, three years $24.00 (add $4.00 per year for foreign postage). Libraries and institutions: $15.00 per year. The International Issue constitutes Numbers 2 & 3 of Volume V. Single issues of the International issue are available at $8.50 to individuals and $11.00 to libraries and institutions (please add $1.00 each U.S. postage; $3.00 each overseas postage). Regular issues of CALYX are $3.50 each, plus 50¢ postage. Address all correspondence to CALYX, P.O. Box B, Corvallis, Oregon 97330. Telephone (503) 753-9384.

The next regular issue of CALYX is scheduled for June 1981. Deadline for submission is March 1, 1981. All submissions received since October 1980 will be considered for that issue.

CALYX accepts submissions of essays, short fiction, poetry and visual art. Prose should not exceed 5,000 words, poetry is limited to six poems, and visual art should be submitted on 35mm slides or 8″ x 10″ black and white glossy photos (limit six slides or photos). Include a brief biographical resume with phone number. All submissions must be accompanied by a stamped self-addressed envelope. CALYX assumes no responsibility for submissions without adequate return postage, packaging and proper identification labels on manuscripts as well as art submissions.

CALYX is indexed in *American Humanities Index*.

Publication costs for this issue were partially funded by matching grants from the National Endowment for the Arts in Washington D.C. (a federal agency), the Coordinating Council of Literary Magazines and the Oregon Arts Commission.

CALYX

A JOURNAL OF ART AND LITERATURE BY WOMEN
INTERNATIONAL ISSUE

October 1980

Managing Editors
Barbara Baldwin
Margarita Donnelly

Assistant Editors
Valerie Eames, Meredith Jenkins,
Anne Krosby, Vicki Shuck

Editorial Board
Barbara Baldwin, Jan Caday, Margarita Donnelly,
Valerie Eames, Meredith Jenkins, Anne Krosby, Vicki Shuck

Contributing Editors
Eva Bowman, Olga Broumas, Meredith Kaplan,
Sharon Olds, Ingrid Wendt, Eleanor Wilner

Cover: Autorretrato con changuito (Self-Portrait with Little Monkey)
Frida Kahlo, oil on canvas
Reprinted with permission of Sra. Dolores Olmedo, Mexico City
Cover Design: John Subert

CALYX was founded in 1976 by
Barbara Baldwin, Margarita Donnelly, Meredith Jenkins and Beth McLagan

CONTENTS

INTRODUCTION

This issue marks the fifth anniversary of CALYX and celebrates a new dimension for this journal of art and literature by women. The editors of CALYX have consistently selected material by women of divergent political, social and personal points of view. However, we have heretofore published only the work of contemporary, North American artists and writers.

When Sharon Olds asked us to consider translations of the Polish poet Wislawa Szymborska, and Nancy Breslow wrote us about her work on Frida Kahlo, several other writers had mentioned translations in progress and we decided to devote an issue of CALYX to work by women in other countries. Announcement of the plan brought a response far beyond our expectations. We glimpsed a portion of the enormous energy being given to the task of translating and publishing the work of women artists previously neglected or unavailable to audiences in this country.

Among the manuscripts we received were translations of work by women like Sor Juana Inés de la Cruz, and Edith Södergran, whose writing was neglected, or met with censure and critical disdain during their lifetimes. Others were translations of contemporary writers like Thelma Nava and Margarita Michelena, who have achieved a measure of acclaim in their own country, but whose poems were excluded from an English translation of the Spanish anthology in which they originally appeared. Although the poems of Anna de Noailles were a literary success when first published, they are no longer included in collections of poetry from that period. Until recently, Frida Kahlo's work was eclipsed by that of her husband, Diego Rivera. The story is familiar and the list is long.

As we worked with these manuscripts, we developed a deeper appreciation of the difficulties that have always confronted women artists seeking to translate those experiences and perceptions unique to female reality into aesthetic forms and structures other than those established in societies dominated by men. So that our readers could share our experience as much as possible, we decided to publish a broad selection of pieces from many different periods and countries. To faithfully represent the artists' voices, and to encompass the scope of the work, we felt compelled to publish a dual-language volume more than three times the normal length of CALYX. Because the ideas and feelings explored by the artists seemed to fall into natural divisions, we have arranged the material loosely according to theme rather than chronological or geographical order.

The artists included here are from tenth century China, eighteenth century Spain, revolutionary Russia and native North America as well as modern Central and South America, Europe, Scandinavia and the middle East. Their themes range

from political struggle and romantic love to creativity and death. Yet what is remarkable about this selection is the common thread of womanhood, of artist as woman speaking from and to a female sensibility regardless of the social, political or historical milieu in which the work originated.

The editors are indebted to everyone who submitted translations and slides and to the many individuals whose unfailing generousity and cooperation helped make this issue possible. We especially want to express our appreciation to Louis Olivier, Department of Foreign Languages, Illinois State University; Miller Williams, President, American Translators Association; Laura Rice-Sayer, Department of English, Oregon State University; and Mary Frances Donnelly-Johnson, Bilingual Specialist, Redwood City Public Library, for their availability as consultants on this issue. For advice and assistance with foreign languages and the myriad details of dual-language publication, we wish to thank Molly Beckley, Richard Dankleff, Bob Frank, Kathy Kerr, Cheryl McLean, Linda Morgan, Miriam Orzech, Zev Orzech, Fred Pfeil, Yang Toa Ping, Cindy Ragland, Karen Ratte, Joyce Shane, Ming Chu Suen, Christian Stehre, Barre Toelken, Gene Van Troyer, Maria Ungier, Leon Ungier, Pedro Wesche and Elliot Zeiss.

The Editors
Corvallis, October 1980

SEARCH FOR MY TONGUE

Days my tongue slips away
I can't hold on to my tongue
it's slippery like the lizard's tail
I try to grasp
but the lizard darts away —

મારી જીભ સરકી જાય છે –

(mari jeebh sarki jai chay —)
I can't speak — I speak nothing.
Nothing —

કાઈ નહિ – હું નથી બોલી શકતી

(Kai nahi — hoo nathi boli shakti)
I search for my tongue —

પરંતુ ક્યાં શોધુ ? ક્યાં ?

(parantu kya shodhu? Kya?)

હું દોડતી દોડતી જાઉ છું –

(hoo dhodti dhodti jaoo choo)
But where should I start? Where?
I go running, running —

નદી કિનારે પહોંચી છું, નદી કિનારે –

(nadi keenaray pohchee choo, nadi keenaray)
reach the river's edge . . .
Silence — એકદમ શાંત .

(Akedum shant)

નીચે પાણી નહિ, ઉપર પક્ષી નહિ –

(neechay pani nahi, oopur pakshi nahi —)
below, the riverbed is dry — above
the sky is empty: no clouds, no birds.
If there were leaves, or even grass
they would not stir today,
for there is no breeze.
If there were clouds
then, it might rain —

જો વાદળા હોત તો કદાચ વરસાદ આવે

(Jo vadla hoat toh kadach varsad aavay)

જો વરસાદ પડે તો નદી પાછી આવે

(jo varsad puday toh nadi pachee aavay)

જો નદી હોય, જો પાણી હોય તો કાઈક લીલું લીલું દેખાય –
(jo nadi hoy, jo pani hoy toh kaeek leelu leelu daykhai)
if the rains fell
then the river might return
if the water rose again I might see something green
at first — then trees enough to fill a forest . . .
If there were some clouds that is —
જો વાદળા હોત તો –
(jo vadla hoat toh)
Since I have lost my tongue
I can only imagine
there is something crawling
beneath the rocks, now burrowing down
into the earth when I lift the rock
જ્યારે પથ્થર ઉપાડુ
(jyaray patther oopadu)
the rock is in my hand, and the dry
moss stuck on the rock
prickles my palm —
I let it drop
for I must find my tongue.
I know it can't be here
in this dry riverbed —
my tongue can only be
where there is water . . .
પાણી . . . પાણી . . .
(pani . . . pani . . .)
કેમ યાદ છે પેલી છોકરી
(hujoo yad chay paylee chokri)
"ઠંડા પાણી . . . મીઠા પાણી . . ." બોલતી બોલતી આવતી –
("thunda pani . . . meetha pani . . ." bolti bolti aavti —)
માથે કાળુ માટલુ, હાથમા પીત્તળનો પ્યાલો –
(mathay kallu matlu, hathma pittulno pyalo)
ઉભેલી ગાડી બાજુ આવતી
(oobhaylee gaadi baju aavti)
બારી તરફ હાથ લંબાવીને પાણી આપતી
(bari taraf hath lumbavenay pani aapti)
અને હું, અતિશય તરસી,
(unay hoo, ateeshay tarsi)

મોટા મોટા ઘૂંટડા લેતી પી જતી –
(mota mota ghuntada layti pee jati)
હુજુ યાદ છે પેલી છોકરી . . .
(hujoo yad chay paylee chokri)
Even water is scarce —
there was a little girl
who carried a black clay pitcher on her head,
who sold water at the train station
she filled her brass cup with water —
stretched out her arm to me,
reached up to the window, up
to me leaning out the window from the train —
but I can't think of her in English.

II

You ask me what I mean
by saying I have lost my tongue —
I ask you, what would you do
if you had two tongues in your mouth,
and lost the first one, the mother tongue,
and could not really know the other,
the foreign tongue —
You could not use them both together
even if you thought that way.
And if you lived in a place where you had to
speak a foreign tongue —
your mother tongue would rot,
rot and die in your mouth
until you had to spit it out.
I thought I spit it out
but overnight while I dream . . .
મને હતુ કે આખી જીભ આખી ભાષા,
(munay hutoo kay aakhee jeebh aakhee bhasha)
મેં થૂંકી નાખી છે.
(may thoonky nakhi chay)
પરંતુ રાત્રે સ્વપ્નામાં મારી ભાષા પાછી આવે છે –
(parantoo rattray svupnama mari bhasha pachi aavay chay)
ફૂલની જેમ મારી ભાષા મારી જીભ
(foolnee jaim mari bhasha mari jeebh)

11

મોઢમાં ખીલે છે –
(moddhama kheelay chay)
ફુલ્લની જેમ મારી ભાષા મારી જીભ
(fulllnee jaim mari bhasha mari jeebh)
મોઢમાં પાકે છે –
(moddhama pakay chay)
it grows back — a stump of a shoot
grows longer, grows moist, grows strong veins,
it ties the other tongue in knots —
the bud opens, the bud opens in my mouth,
it pushes the other tongue aside.
Everytime I think I have forgotten,
I think I have lost the mother tongue —
it blossoms out of my mouth —
Days I try to think in English:
I look up, પેલો કાળો કાગડો
(paylo kallo kagdo)
ઉડતો ઉડતો જાય, હવે ઝાડે પહોંચે,
(oodto oodto jai, huhvay jzaday pohchay)
એની ચાંચમાં કાંઈક છે –
(ainee chanchma kaeek chay)
the crow has something in his beak.
When I look up
I think: આકાશ, સુરજ
(aakash, suraj)
and then: sky, sun —
Don't tell me it is the same, I know
better — to think of the sky
is to think of dark clouds bringing snow,
the first snow is always on Thanksgiving.
But to think: આકાશ, અસમાન, આભ
(aakash, usman, aabh)
માથે મોટા કાળા કાગડા ઉડે
(mathay mota kalla kagda ooday)
કાગડાને માથે સુરજ, રોજે સુરજ
(kagdanay mathay suraj, rojay suraj)
એકપણ વાદળ નહિ, અતેલય વરસાદ નહિ
(akepun vadul nahi, atelay varsad nahi)

અટલે અનાજ નહિ, અટલે રોટલી નહિ
(atelay anaj nahi, atelay rotli nahi)
દાળ ભાત શાક નહિ, કાંઈ નહિ, કૂછ બી નહિ
(dhal bhat shak nahi, kai nahi, kooch be nahi)
માત્ર કાગડા, કાળા કાગડા —
(matra kagda, kalla kagda —)
Overhead, large black crows fly —
over the crows, the sun, always
the sun, not a single cloud
which means no rain, which means no wheat
no rice, no greens, no bread — Nothing
only crows, black crows.
And yet, the humid June air,
the stormiest sky in Connecticut
can never be: આકાશ
          (aakash)
ચોમાસામાં જ્યારે વરસાદ આવે
(chomasama jyaray varsad aavay)
આખી રાત આખો દી' વરસાદ પડે — વિજળી જાય
(aakhee raat aakho dee varsad puday — vijli jai)
જ્યારે મા રસોડામાં ઘીને દીવે રોટલી વણતી
(jyaray ma rasodama gheenay deevay rotli vanti)
શાક હલાવતી
(shak halavti)
રવીન્દ્રસંગીત ગાતી ગાતી
(Ravindrasangeet gaati gaati)
સૌને બોલાવતી.
(saonay bolavti)
the monsoon sky giving rain
all night, all day — lightning — the electricity goes out,
we light the cotton wicks in butter:
          candles in brass —
and my mother in the kitchen
my mother singing:
મોનો મોરો મેઘેરો શૂંગે, ઉડે ચાલે દીક દી ગોંતરો પાની . . .
(mono moro meghero shoongay, ooday chalay deek de gontayro pani . . .)
I can't hear my mother in English.

13

III

In the middle of Maryland
you send me a tape recording
saying: "કહે આ એક વાત તો કહેવીજ પડશે,
    (huhvay aa ake vaat toh kahveej padshay)
ભલેનય બહાર કૂતરા ભસે, ભલે ધોબી આવે
(bhalaynay bahr kootra bhasay, bhalay dhobi aavay)
ભલે શાકવાળી આવે, મારે આ વાત તો કહેવીજ પડશો
(bhalay shakvali aavay, maray aa vat toh kahveej padshay)
ભલે તપાલી આવે, ભલે કાગડા કૉ કૉ કરે
(bhalay tapali aavay, bhalay kagda kaw kaw karay)
ભલે રીકશાનો અવાજ આવે
(bhalay rickshano avaj aavay)
મારે તને આ વાત તો કહેવીજ પડશે."
(maray tanay aa vat toh kahveej padshay)
You talk to me,
     you say my name the way it should be said
apologising
for the dogs barking outside
for the laundryman knocking on the door
apologising because
the woman selling egg plants
is crying રીંગણા ... રીંગણા ...   door to door
     (reengna . . . reengna . . .)
but do you know
how I miss that old woman, crying રીંગણા ... રીંગણા ...
                    (reengna . . . reengna . . .)
It's alright if the peddlar's brass bells ring out
I miss them too —
You talk louder, the mailman comes, knocking louder —
the crows caw caw cawing outside
the rickshaw's motor put-put-puttering . . .
you say: સુજુ બેન કહે તમારે માટે તબલા વગાડુ છું.
     (Suju bhen huhvay tamaray matay tabla vagadu choo)
you say: listen to the tablas —
listen: ધા ધીન ધીન ધા *(dha dhin dhin dha)*

14

ધા ધિન ધિન ધા   *(dha dhin dhin dha)*

listen ધા ધિન ધિન ધા   *(dha dhin dhin dha)*

ધિનક ધિનક ધિન ધિન   *(dhinaka dhinaka dhin dhin)*

ધિનક ધિનક ધિન ધિન   *(dhinaka dhinaka dhin dhin)*

ધા ધિન ધિન ધા   *(dha dhin dhin dha)*

ધિનક ધિનક ધિનક ધિનક   *(dhinaka dhinaka dhinaka dhinaka)*

ધા ધિન ધિન ધા   *(dha dhin dhin dha)*

ધિનક ધિનક ધિન ધિન   *(dhinaka dhinaka dhin dhin)*

I listen   I listen   I listen

ધા ધિન ધિન ધા   *(dha dhin dhin dha)*

I hear you   I hear you

ધિનક ધિનક ધિન ધિનક ધિનક ધિન ધિનક ધિનક ધિન

(dhinaka dhinaka dhin dhinaka dhinaka dhin dhinaka dhinaka dhin)

listen   listen   listen

Today I played your tape

over and over again

ધા ધિન ધિન ધા   *(dha dhin dhin dha)*

ધિનક ધિનક ધા   *(dhinaka dhinaka dha)*

                                 I can't ધા *(dha)*

I can't ધા *(dha)*

I can't forget   I can't forget

ધા ધિન ધિન ધા *(dha dhin dhin dha)*

Sujata P. Bhatt

Zuleyka Benitez

pencil 18" x 24"

The Private Joke

16

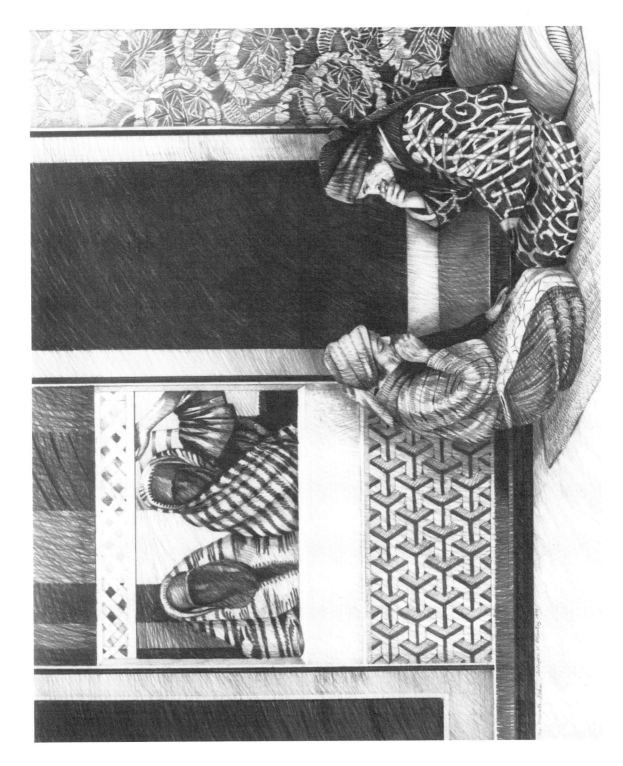

The Seduction of the Chihuahuas

pencil 18" x 20"

Zuleyka Benitez

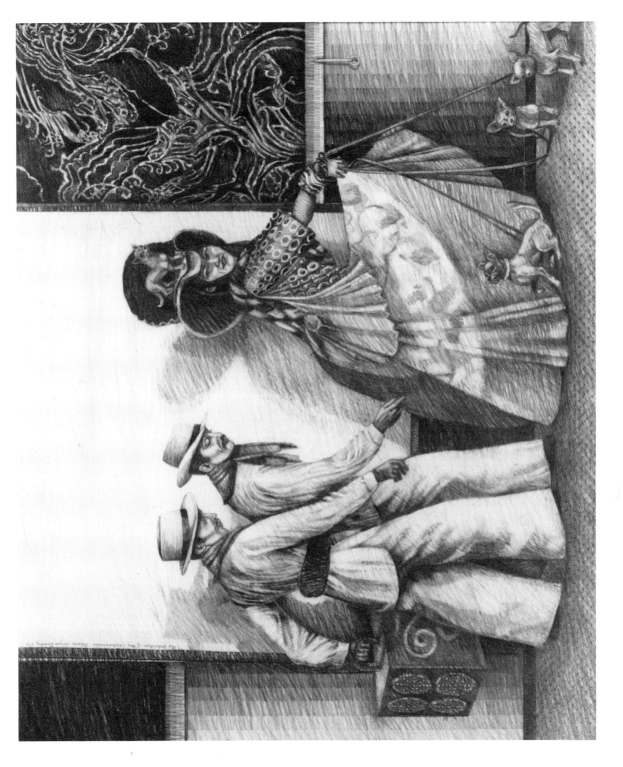

Zuleyka Benitez

Small-Footed Ladies of the S.L.A. Moments Before the End

pencil 18" x 24"

WRITTEN AFTER HEARING
ABOUT THE SOVIET INVASION OF AFGHANISTAN —

Here,
a child born
in winter
    rarely survives —
Bibi Jamal's son died.
She pounds hard dough,
quickly kneads in yak milk, kneads in fat.
Rolls the dough out round and flat —
her older co-wife cooks the bread.
Bibi Jamal can not speak
of it yet . . .

It is cold enough. Birds have come inside;
her co-wife sleeps now, thick feet
by the fire in the yurt's center.
On the fire's other side Bibi Jamal weaves
the world of Darjeeling into a carpet:
    hills sprouting tea leaves, rivers froth down mountains
    and there must be red, she feels,
    long red skirts flowing through fields,
    ripe pomegranates broken open in some garden . . .
    with such green
    with that blue Himalayan sky
                there is always red.
nothing like
the granite, treeless
mountains she knows.

Bibi Jamal's thread never breaks
even as she dreams of Darjeeling
and her husband — already on the Hindu Kush —
does not know
how her breasts ache with milk.

She can hear
    his voice slice through icy gusts —
    caravanserai well water sweet on his tongue . . .
    she listens: snow falls
    her husband pitches his black tent;
    nearby she spots
    a slouched snow leopard
    now it moves, startles her —
    pauses, sniffs the air, steals
    away through sharp sword grass.
    Her husband remains
    safe in his black tent . . .
Soon he will be beyond the Khyber pass —
she draws green thread through her fingers . . .

        -2-
What do you know of Bibi Jamal?
Her husband napalmed,
                          ran burning across the rocks . . .
crisp shreds of skin, a piece of his turban,
a piece of his skull were delivered
to her — she only stared
did not understand
muttered, "Allah Allah Allah Allah is great . . . but
where is my husband? Allah Allah Allah . . ."
She will ask you when she understands.

Sujata P. Bhatt

ESTELÍ

Estelí
río del Este
después de cuarenta años
de sequía
de despojos
de burla
de césares rapaces
se ha llenado tu cauce.
Con lodo y sangre
se ha llenado
con cartuchos vacíos
y con sangre
con camisas
pantalones
y cadáveres
pegándose como algas
a las rocas.
Un hedor sofocante
emana de tu río.
Estelí
río del Este
tus náufragos no pueden ocuparse
caminan cabizbajos
merodean
buscan en los escombros
esas tijeras rotas
esa máquina Singer

ESTELÍ

Estelí
Eastern river
after forty years
of drought
of plunder
of deception
of predatory rulers
your bed no longer dry.
With slime and blood
it has been filled
with empty cartridges
and with blood
and shirts
pants
and corpses
sticking like algae
to the rocks.
A suffocating stench
rises from the river.
Estelí
Eastern river
your shipwrecked can't find employment
they walk downcast
marauding
searching the rubble
for those broken scissors
that Singer sewing machine

El río Estelí
está chorreando sangre
y fueron tus hijastros
tus hijastros vestidos
de guardias nacionales
tus hijastros desatados
por Somoza
adiestrados
amaestrados
y castrados
por Somoza
y mercenarios lucrados
de Somoza
tus hijastros mal pagados
por el hijastro Somoza
los que lanzaron fuego
y destruyeron.
Estelí,
río del Este
estás llorando sangre.

Claribel Alegría

26

The river Estelí
is spurting blood
and it was your step-sons
your step-sons dressed
as national guards
your step-sons unleashed
by Somoza
trained
tamed
by Somoza
and castrated
and mercenaries hired
by Somoza
your step-sons underpaid
by step-son Somoza
who opened fire
and destroyed
Estelí
Eastern river
you are weeping blood.

Claribel Alegría
translated by *Electa Arenal* and *Marsha Gabriela Dreyer*

El tiempo que no he tenido el cielo azul
y sus nubes gordas de algodón en rama,
sabe que el dolor del exilio
ha hecho florecer cipreses en mi carne.
Es dolor el recuerdo de la tierra mojada,
la lectura diaria del periódico
que dice que suceden
cada vez más atrocidades,
que mueren y caen presos los amigos
que desaparecen los campesinos
como tragados por la montaña.

Es dolor este moverme en las calles
con nombres de otros días, otras batallas,
de otros personajes que no son de mi historia.
Es dolor caminar entre caras desconocidas
con quienes no puedo compartir un poema,
hablar de cosas de la familia
o simplemente despotricar contra el gobierno.

Es dolor llegar hasta el borde,
ver de lejos el lago,
los rótulos en la carretera: Frontera de Nicaragua
y saber que aún no se puede llegar más allá,
que lo más que se puede es empinarse
y tratar de sentir el olor de las flores y campos y quemas.

Es dolor, pero se crece en canto
porque el dolor es fértil como la alegría
riega, se riega por dentro,
enseña cosas insospechadas
enseña rabias
y viene floreciendo en tantas caras
que a punta de dolor
es seguro que pariremos
un amanecer
para esta noche larga.

Gioconda Belli

28

They who don't know that at this point
grief is also a famous last name. . .
                              Mario Benedetti

The time that has passed since I have seen a blue sky
with its heavy clouds of raw cotton
knows that the pain of exile
has made cypresses flower in my body.
I grieve at the memory of damp earth,
the daily reading of the newspaper
that says that more atrocities
happen each day,
that friends fall prisoner and die
that peasants disappear
as if swallowed by the mountain.

I grieve moving in these streets
with names of other days, other battles,
of other celebrities that are not a part of my history.
I grieve walking among unknown faces
with whom I cannot share a poem,
talk of family matters
or simply rail against the government.

I grieve arriving at the border
seeing the lake from afar,
the signs on the highway: Nicaraguan Frontier
and knowing that you still can not go farther,
that the most you can do is lean forward
and try to smell the scent of flowers and fields and fires.

It is grief,
but it grows into song
because grief is fertile — like happiness
it waters, waters from within,
grief teaches the unsuspected,
it teaches rage
and flowers in many faces
for by dint of grief
we are certain to give birth to
a dawn
for this long night.

Gioconda Belli
translated by *Marsha Gabriela Dreyer* and *Electa Arenal*

FREEDOM NOW
       a la lucha de los negros en los Estados Unidos
                              al SNCC

en el sur de los Estados Unidos
se fabrican ferrocarriles ganchos lámparas
ganchos pintura de uña para señoritas
cremas y helados de chocolate
tinte plateado autos edificios de propiedad horizontal
        televisores escuelas democráticas

se celebra Halloween en Estados Unidos
hay también Alabama Mississippi
        Texas
        la gran Texas rubita y pedigüeña
Birmingham Virginia
        New Orleans – gargajo de los Louises con Mardi
                Gras y todo

es decir
ciudades misteriosas llenas de gente
que lincha negros y pisa cucarachas
cualquier vaca sureña exclamaría orgullosa:
"en estos tiempos de Coca-cola
fuerza nuclear y conferencias internacionales
vale mucho más mi leche
que el semen de un estudiante negro"

Nancy Morejón

30

FREEDOM NOW
To the Black struggle in the United States
to SNCC

in the South of the United States
they make trains hooks lamps
hooks fingernail polish for women
face creams and chocolate icecream
silver dye cars buildings of horizontal ownership
        televisions democratic schools

Halloween is celebrated in the United States
and also Alabama Mississippi
        Texas
        big blond consuming Texas
Birmingham Virginia
        New Orleans — the phlegm of the louis with Mardi
                Gras and everything

it is to say
mysterious cities full of people
who lynch Blacks and step on roaches
any southern cow would proudly exclaim:
"in these times of Coca-cola
nuclear power and international conferences
my milk is worth much more
than a black student's sperm"

Nancy Morejón
translated by *Kay Boulware-Miller*

KINSEY REPORT

1.   – ¿Si soy casada? Sí. Esto quiere decir
     que se levantó un acta en alguna oficina
     y se volvió amarilla con el tiempo
     y que hubo ceremonia en una iglesia
     con padrinos y todo. Y el banquete
     y la semana entera en Acapulco.

     No, ya no puedo usar mi vestido de boda.
     He subido de peso con los hijos,
     con las preocupaciones. Ya usted ve, no faltan.

     Con frecuencia, que puedo predecir,
     mi marido hace uso de sus derechos o,
     como él gusta llamarlo, paga el débito
     conyugal. Y me da la espalda. Y ronca.

     Yo me resisto siempre. Por decoro.
     Pero, siempre también, cedo. Por obediencia.

     No, no me gusta nada.
     De cualquier modo no debería de gustarme
     porque yo soy decente ¡y él es tan material!

     Además, me preocupa otro embarazo.
     Y esos jadeos fuertes y el chirrido
     de los resortes de la cama pueden
     despertar a los niños que no duermen después
     hasta la madrugada.

2.   Soltera, sí. Pero no virgen. Tuve
     un primo a los trece años.

     El de catorce y no sabíamos nada.
     Me asusté mucho. Fuí con un doctor
     que me dió algo y no hubo consecuencias.

     Ahora soy mecanógrafa y algunas veces salgo
     a pasear con amigos.
     Al cine y a cenar. Y terminamos
     la noche en un motel. Mi mamá no se entera.

     Al principio me daba vergüenza, me humillaba
     que los hombres me vieran de ese modo
     después. Que me negaran
     el derecho a negarme cuando no tenía ganas
     porque me habían fichado como puta.

KINSEY REPORT

1.   — Am I a married woman? Yes, I mean
        somebody made out a license in some office
        in time it turned yellow
        and there was a church ceremony
        with sponsors and everything. And a banquet
        and a whole week in Acapulco.

        No, I can't wear my wedding dress anymore.
        I've put on weight with the children
        and the problems. As you can see, there's enough of those.

        At a rate I can regularly predict
        my husband makes use of his rights,
        or as he likes to say, he pays the conjugal
        debt. Then he turns his back on me and snores.

        I always resist. Out of decency.
        But then I always give in. Out of obedience.

        No, I don't like anything special
        Anyhow I'm not supposed to like it.
        Because I'm a decent woman; and he's so gross!

        Besides, I worry about getting pregnant again.
        And the panting and the squeaking of the
        bedsprings might wake up the children
        who won't go back to sleep until dawn

2.   Single, yes. But not a virgin. There was
        my cousin when I was thirteen.
        He was fourteen and we didn't know about anything.
        I got very scared. I went to a doctor
        who gave me something and nothing happened.

        Now I'm a typist and sometimes I go out
        with my men friends.
        To the movies or to dinner. We end up spending
        the night at a motel. My mother ignores it.

        At first I was ashamed, it humiliated me
        to have men look at me that way *afterwards.*
        To deny me the right to say no when I didn't feel like it
        because they had me tagged as a whore.

Y ni siquiera cobro. Y ni siquiera
puedo tener caprichos en la cama.

Son todos unos tales. ¿Que que por qué lo hago?
Porque me siento sola. O me fastidio.

Porque ¿no lo ve usted? estoy envejeciendo.
Ya perdí la esperanza de casarme
y prefiero una que otra cicatriz
a tener la memoria como un cofre vacío.

3. Divorciada. Porque era tan mula como todos.
    Conozco a muchos más. Por eso es que comparo.

    De cuando en cuando echo una cana al aire
    para no convertirme en una histérica.

    Pero tengo que dar el buen ejemplo
    a mis hijas. No quiero que su suerte
    se parezca a la mía.

4. Tengo ofrecida a Dios esta abstinencia
    ¡por caridad, no entremos en detalles!

    A veces sueño. A veces despierto derramándome
    y me cuesta un trabajo decirle al confesor
    que, otra vez, he caído porque la carne es flaca.

    Ya dejé de ir al cine. La oscuridad ayuda
    y la aglomeración en los elevadores.

    Creyeron que me iba a volver loca
    pero me está atendiendo un médico. Masajes.

    Y me siento mejor.

5. A los indispensables (como ellos se creen)
    los puede usted echar a la basura,
    como hicimos nosotras.

    Mi amiga y yo nos entendemos bien.
    Y la que manda es tierna, como compensación;
    así como también, la que obedece,
    es coqueta y se toma sus revanchas.

I don't even charge. I can't even
get a few kicks in bed.

They're all s.o.b.'s. What do you mean, why do I do it?
Because I feel lonely. Or I get fed up.

Because, can't you see? I'm getting old.
I've lost hopes of getting married
and I'd rather have a couple of scars
than a memory like an empty hopechest.

3.   Divorced. Because he was stupid like all the rest of them.
     I know a lot of other men. That's why I can compare.

     Once in a while I go on a fling
     so I won't get hysterical.

     But I have to set a good example
     for my daughters. I don't want them
     to repeat my luck.

4.   I've offered this abstinence up to God.
     Please, let's not go into details.

     Sometimes I dream. Sometimes I wake up all wet
     and it's really hard to tell my confessor that
     I've sinned again because the flesh is weak.

     I don't go to the movies anymore. The darkness
     and the crowds in the elevators make it worse.

     They thought I was going to go crazy
     but a doctor is treating me. Massages.

     And I'm feeling better.

5.   You can just throw the indispensable sex
     (as they like to believe themselves)
     into the garbage, the way we did.

     My girlfriend and I get along very well.
     The one who dominates is tender, in compensation;

Vamos a muchas fiestas, viajamos a menudo
y en el hotel pedimos
un solo cuarto y una sola cama.

Se burlan de nosotras pero también nosotras
nos burlamos de ellos y quedamos a mano.

Cuando nos aburramos de estar solas
alguna de las dos irá a agenciarse un hijo.

¡No, no de esa manera! En el laboratorio
de la inseminación artificial.

6. Señorita. Sí, insisto. Señorita.

Soy joven. Dicen que no fea. Carácter
llevadero. Y un día
vendrá el Príncipe Azul, porque se lo he rogado
como un milagro a San Antonio. Entonces
vamos a ser felices. Enamorados siempre.

¿Qué importa la pobreza? Y si es borracho
lo quitaré del vicio. Si es un mujeriego
yo voy a mantenerme siempre tan atractiva,
tan atenta a sus gustos, tan buena ama de casa,
tan prolífica madre
y tan extraordinaria cocinera
que se volverá fiel como premio a mis méritos
entre los que, el mayor, es la paciencia.

Lo mismo que mis padres y los de mi marido
celebraremos nuestras bodas de oro
con gran misa solemne.

No, no he tenido novio. No, ninguno
todavía. Mañana.

Rosario Castellanos

We go to a lot of parties, we travel a lot
and at the hotels we ask for
a single room with one bed.

They laugh at us but we laugh at them too
so we're even.

When we get bored with being by ourselves
one of us is going to get a baby from an agency.

No, not that way! From an artificial
insemination lab.

6.   Miss. Yes, I insist, Miss.

I'm young. They say I'm not bad-looking. Easy-going
disposition. And one day
my Prince will come, because I've prayed to Saint Anthony
to get him for me. Then
we'll be happy. Sweethearts forever.

What does it matter if we're poor? If he drinks
I'll cure him of it. If he chases women
I'm just going to keep myself always so attractive,
so attentive to his tastes, such a good housewife,
such a prolific mother
and such a great cook
that he'll become faithful as a prize for my merits
among which the greatest is patience.

We'll celebrate our golden wedding anniversary
with a solemn high mass
just like my parents and my husband's parents.

No, I've never had a boyfriend. No, none
yet. Tomorrow.

Rosario Castellanos
translated by *Maureen Ahern*

2પ5 dl

(Uhdaylee)*
*only paper and wood are safe
from a menstruating woman's touch*

I have spent the day in such idleness!
sketching banyan trees:
the rough bark, the long branches
sending out shoots to the ground,
those strong vines we swung on
when we were children
holding on even though the bark bruised our palms —
swinging out in a wide arc
far out of the dark canopy of hanging roots —
we would swing out to the sky, then leap down,
leap-frogging across the wet grass . . .
Oh I have spent the day
in such idleness with my water colors,
filling my wide sheets of paper
with spider lilies, snapdragons, zinnias . . .

Now there is such darkness outside
the new moon
thick haze swathing the stars —
bats fly squealing past my window,
the spiders leave, crawling out on the ledge
as if they know I am untouchable.
The wind comes whistling after the bats
as I turn to light my kerosene lamp —
but who can read on a night like this
I can't leave the window — but stand
listening to this new moon blackness:
crickets cricketing, something buzzing —
now the bullfrogs' watery gurgle begins . . .

My second night —
itching to get back to my knitting — I pace
in this small room, I pace from my narrow bed to the book shelf
filled with dusty newspapers —
glossy brown cowries surrounding a conch —
then, holding the conch shell to my ear
I can feel my blood flowing
a dull throbbing
a slow drumming within my head, my hips —
this aching is my blood flowing against, rushing against, my blood
roaring the ocean's roar
trapped deep within me — rises,
blood churning out of my ocean bed rises —
knotted clumps of my blood,
I remember fistfuls of torn sea weed rising with the foam,
rising — then falling, falling up on the sand
strewn over newly laid turtle eggs —
and so I ache — all night I ache . . .

Sujata P. Bhatt

★ અછડેલ *(Uhdaylee) means "untouchable when one is menstruating."*

Daina Dagnija

oil on canvas 72" x 84"

The Village Who Fled

Daina Dagnija

oil on canvas 72" x 70"

The Flea Market

* * *

czasem
stęskniona okrutnie
pojawiam się ludziom
w mojej dawnej twarzy
idę na moich dawnych stopach

i dotykam ich z uśmiechem
dawnymi rękoma

ale zdradza mnie
przejrzystość skóry
przypominającej strukturę papieru
i nieruchomość cienia
i po przejściu moim
brak najlżejszego śladu na śniegu

i nagle porażeni wiedzą
rozsuwają się wylęknieni
ofiarując mi wielką białą przestrzeń
bez horyzontu

Halina Poswiatowska

* * *

sometimes
too full of longing
I come to people
in my old face
I walk on my old feet
I smile and touch them
with my old hands

what betrays me
is my transparent skin
its paper texture
and the immobility of my shadow
and the lack of footprints
after I cross the snow

they suddenly understand
and draw aside, afraid
offering me an expanse of white
with no horizon

Halina Poswiatowska
translated by *Grazýna Drabik* and *Sharon Olds*

TÚ ME QUIERES BLANCA

Tú me quieres alba,
Me quieres de espumas,
Me quieres de nácar.
Que sea azucena
Sobre todas, casta.
De perfume tenue.
Corola cerrada.

Ni un rayo de luna
Filtrado me haya.
Ni una margarita
Se diga mi hermana.
Tú me quieres nívea,
Tú me quieres blanca,
Tú me quieres alba.

Tú que hubiste todas
Las copas a mano,
De frutos y mieles
Los labios morados.
Tú que en el banquete
Cubierto de pámpanos
Dejaste las carnes
Festejando a Baco.
Tú que en los jardines
Negros del Engaño
Vestido de rojo
Corriste al Estrago.

Tú que el esqueleto
Conservas intacto
No sé todavía
Por cuáles milagros
Me pretendes blanca
(Dios te lo perdone),
Me pretendes casta
(Dios te lo perdone),
¡Me pretendes alba!

YOU WANT ME WHITE

You want me pure,
You want me made of froth,
Made of mother-of-pearl.
I should be a lily
Above all, chaste.
Of tenuous perfume.
Corolla closed.

Not even a ray of the moon
Should have penetrated me.
Nor a daisy
Call herself my sister.
You want me like the snow,
You want me white,
You want me pure.

You who have
Drunk from every cup,
Your lips stained
With fruit and honey.
You who have abandoned your flesh
Celebrating Bacchus
At vine-covered tables.
You who in the
Black gardens of deceit
Dressed in red
Rushed to corruption.

You who still have
Your skeleton intact
I don't know
Through what miracle,
You want me white
(God forgive you)
You want me chaste
(God forgive you)
You want me pure!

Huye hacia los bosques;
Vete a la montaña;
Límpiate la boca;
Vive en las cabañas;
Toca con las manos
La tierra mojada;
Alimenta el cuerpo
Con raíz amarga;
Bebe de las rocas;
Duerme sobre escarcha;
Renueva tejidos
Con salitre y agua;
Habla con los pájaros
Y lévate al alba.
Y cuando las carnes
Te sean tornadas,
Y cuando hayas puesto
En ellas el alma
Que por las alcobas
Se quedó enredada,
Entonces, buen hombre,
Preténdeme blanca,
Preténdeme nívea,
Preténdeme casta.

Alfonsina Storni

Flee to the woods;
Get yourself to the mountain;
Clean your mouth;
Live in huts;
Touch the damp earth
With your hands;
Nourish your body
With bitter roots;
Drink from the rocks;
Sleep on the frost;
Renew your tissue
With salt and water;
Speak to the birds
And rise at dawn.
And when your flesh
Is returned to you,
And when you have put
Back into it the soul
You've left around
In bedrooms,
Then, my good man,
Ask that I be white,
Ask that I be like the snow,
Ask that I be chaste.

Alfonsina Storni
translated by *Almitra David*

EL VELO CENTELLEANTE

I   Yo no canto
por dejar testimonio de mi paso,
ni para que me escuchen los que, conmigo, mueren,
ni por sobrevivirme en las palabras.
Canto para salir de mi rostro en tinieblas
a recordar los muros de mi casa,
porque entrando en mis ojos quedé ciega
y a tientas reconozco, cuando canto,
el infinito umbral de mi morada.

II   Cuando me separaste de ti, cuando me diste
el país de mi cuerpo, y me alejaste
del jardín de tus manos,
yo tuve, en prenda tuya, las palabras,
temblorosos espejos donde, a veces,
sorprendo tus señales.
Sólo tengo palabras. Sólo tengo
mi voz infiel para buscarte.

Reino oscuro de enigmas me entregaste.
y un ángel que me hiere cuando te olvido y callo.
Y una lengua doliente y una copa sellada.
Esto es la poesía. No un don de fácil música
ni una gracia riente.
Apenas una forma de recordar. Apenas
– entre el hombre y su orilla –
una señal, un puente.
Por él voy con mis pasos,
con mi tiempo y mi muerte,
llevando en estas manos prometidas al polvo
– que de ti me separan, que en otra me convierten –
un hilo misterioso, una escala secreta,
una llave que a veces abre puertas de sombra,
una lejana punta del velo centelleante.

Eso tengo y no más. Una manera
de zarpar por instantes de mi carne,
del límite y del nombre que me diste,
del ser y el tiempo en que me confinaste.

THE OUTCAST

I. I do not sing
    to leave testimony of my journey
    nor so that others, who die with me, will listen,
    nor to live forever in my words.
    I sing to part from my darkened face,
    to imagine the walls of my house
    because, entering, I remained blind,
    and recognize only when I sing
    the infinite threshold of my home.

II. When you left, withdrew
    the garden of your hands, gave back to me
    the country of my body,
    I held, in pawn, words,
    trembling mirrors where sometimes
    I see you.
    I have only words, I have only
    my unfaithful voice with which to find you.
    You left me to a dark kingdom of puzzles
    and an angel that hurts me when, silent, I forget you,
    and an aching tongue and an empty cup.
    This is poetry. Not a gift of easy music
    or a smiling grace.
    Hardly a form to record, hardly,
    between us,
    a bridge, a sign.
    Because of you I come with my footsteps,
    with my time and my death.
    In these hands promised to dust,
    marking separation, that impenetrable frontier,
    mysterious path, hidden stairway,
    I carry a key that opens shadowed doors,
    the faraway tip of the flashing veil.
    This I have and no more: a way
    of travelling beyond my flesh,
    a name you gave me,
    a being and time in which you confined me

Has querido dejarme un torpe vuelo,
la raíz de mis alas anteriores
y este nublado espejo, rastro apenas
de la memoria que me arrebataste.

Y yo, que antes de la ceguera
del nacer, fuí contigo
una sonora gota de tu música inmensa,
lloro bajo la cifra de mi nombre,
en esta soledad de ser yo misma,
de ser entre mi sangre un nostálgico huésped
que su idioma ha olvidado, mas no olvida
que es hoja separada de su ramo celeste.

III Pero voy caminando hacia el retorno.
Pero voy caminando hacia el silencio.
Pero voy caminando hacia tu rostro,
allá donde la musica dejó ya de ser tiempo,
allá donde las voces son todas la voz tuya.

Aún es mi camino de palabras,
aún no me disuelves en tu música,
aún no me confundes y me salvas.
Mas tú me tomarás desde el cadáver
vacío de mis pasos,
derribarás de un soplo la muralla
de mi nombre y mis manos
y apagarás la vacilante antorcha
con que mi voz, abajo, te buscaba.

Recobrarás el incendiado espejo
en que atisbe, temblando, tu fantasma,
y este sonoro sello que en mi frente
me señaló un destino de nostalgia.
Y callaré. Devolveré este reino
a frágiles palabras.
¿Por qué cantar entonces, si ya habré recordado,
si estará abierta entonces esta rosa enigmática?

Margarita Michelena

almost flightless,
awkwardly flapping my fore-wings.
You left me this dark mirror, this theatre
of memory.

And I, who went with you
lost in your resounding ocean,
cry beneath the cipher of my name,
in this solitude of being myself,
of being, inside my blood, a lonely guest
your language has forgotten
but who does not forget,
a leaf of your shining branch.

III.   But I return.
I walk towards silence.
I walk towards your face,
where music falls out of tune,
where all voices are your voice.

This, then, is my road of words.
Although you keep me from your music,
although you refuse me, you save me.
You show me the empty
shape of my footprints;
your sigh knocks over walls,
blows out the flickering torch
of the voice within me,
with which I looked for you.

You will pull out the sword
the angel thrust in my thigh,
rub this scar, betraying my lonely destiny,
off my forehead.
And I will fall. I will return this kingdom
to fragile words.
Then why sing? If I have already imagined,
if it has already opened, this inexplicable rose.

Margarita Michelena
translated by *Nancy Prothro*

ÉQUINOXE

Ce soir, j'ai tout l'automne en moi,
Ses gris, ses désespoirs, ses morts et ses tempêtes,
Et tout le menaçant émoi
Des malfaiteurs de route – oh fières et fortes têtes!
Moi, le déshérité des humains, dont vous êtes,
Volontaire déshérité,
Que vous me faites mal avec votre gaîté!
– Car j'ai quitté toutes vos fêtes.
Prenez garde ! je vous rendrai le mal que vous me faites.
Je suis le Juif errant et le déshérité –
Dieu de ma destinée, et souvent de la tienne,
O femmes, trop diverses : "toi."
Mais, la marque reste seule en moi.
Toi, par le mauvais temps, faut-il qu'il t'en souvienne
– A peine?
Voici venir l'automne, et l'on rentre chez soi:
L'amour familial dans la maison jolie!
Mais nous qui nous chauffons au feu de la folie,
Où donc est notre épaule, où donc est notre toit?
Amants des grands chemins, usons nos bons cerveaux,

Nos bras qui ne savent qu'étreindre.
– Etreindre? Mieux vaudrait étrangler – et sans geindre
Se tuer dans l'égout pour l'amour vieux-nouveau,
La face bien marquée de tous leurs crocs, (répliques
Que nous auront données ces chiennes dites nos soeurs)
Mais la face levée vers le ciel, extatiques,
D'un dernier coup de poing, au coeur!

Natalie Clifford Barney

EQUINOX

　　　Tonight, I have autumn in my soul.
Its gray, despair, its dead and its tempests
　　　And all the threatening emotion
Of highway bandits — stubborn and proud!
Disowned by the human race to which you belong,
　　　I volunteer my separation.
How you hurt me with your gaiety!
　　　— For I abandoned your feasts.
Beware! I will repay wounds inflicted.
I am the wandering Jew and the outcast —
God of my destiny, and often of yours,
　　　O women, "you," of many strains
　　　But the stigma in me alone remains.
You, in bad weather, must the memory linger
　　　— A little?
Here comes the autumn and all go home.
Family love in a pretty house!
But we who warm ourselves at folly's hearth,
Where is our shoulder, where is our roof?
Lovers at crossroads, let's use our brains,
　　　Arms that know only hugs.
— Hugs? Better to strangle with no moans
Suicide in the sewer for old-and-new love,
Faces bitten by those called our sisters
Responding like bitches with canine teeth
But faces lifted to the sky ecstatic,
　　　With a last punch in the heart!

Natalie Clifford Barney
translated by *Pauline Newman-Gordon*

PRZY WINIE

Spojrzał, dodał mi urody,
a ja wzięłam ją jak swoją.
Szczęśliwa, połknęłam gwiazdę.

Pozwoliłam się wymyślić
na podobieństwo odbicia
w jego oczach. Tańczę, tańczę
w zatrzęsieniu nagłych skrzydeł.

Stół jest stołem, wino winem
w kieliszku, co jest kieliszkiem
i stoi stojąc na stole.
A ja jestem urojona,
urojona nie do wiary,
urojona aż do krwi.

Mówię mu, co chce: o mrówkach
umierających z miłości
pod gwiazdozbiorem dmuchawca.
Przysięgam, że biała róża,
pokropiona winem, śpiewa.

Śmieję się, przechylam głowę
ostrożnie, jakbym sprawdzała
wynalazek. Tańczę, tańczę
w zdumionej skórze, w objęciu
które mnie stwarza.

Ewa z żebra, Venus z piany,
Minerwa z głowy Jowisza
były bardziej rzeczywiste.

DRINKING WINE

He looked, and gave me beauty,
and I took it as if mine.
Happy, I swallowed a star.

I allowed myself to be
invented in the likeness
of the reflection in his eyes.
I am dancing, dancing
in the flutter of sudden wings.

A table is a table,
wine is wine in a glass
that is just a glass and stands
standing on a table. While
I am imaginary
to the point of no belief,
imaginary
to the point of blood.

I am telling him
what he wants to hear: ants
dying of love under
the constellation of the dandelion.
I swear that a white rose,
sprinkled with wine, sings.

I am laughing, tilting
my head carefully
as if checking an invention.
I am dancing, dancing
in astonished skin, in
an embrace that creates me.

Eve from a rib, Venus from sea-foam,
Minerva from Jove's head —
all were more real than I.

Kiedy on nie patrzy na mnie,
szukam swojego odbicia
na ścianie. I widzę tylko
gwóźdź, z którego zdjęto obraz.

Wisława Szymborska

PORTRET KOBIECY

Musi być do wyboru.
Zmieniać się, żeby tylko nic się nie zmieniło.
To łatwe, niemożliwe, trudne, warte próby.
Oczy ma, jeśli trzeba, raz modre, raz szare,
czarne, wesołe, bez powodu pełne łez.
Śpi z nim jak pierwsza z brzegu, jedyna na świecie.
Urodzi mu czworo dzieci, żadnych dzieci, jedno.
Naiwna, ale najlepiej doradzi.
Słaba, ale udźwignie.
Nie ma głowy na karku, to będzie ją miała.
Czyta Jaspersa i pisma kobiece.
Nie wie po co ta śrubka i zbuduje most.
Młoda, jak zwykle młoda, ciągle jeszcze młoda.
Trzyma w rękach wróbelka ze złamanym skrzydłem,
własne pieniądze na podróż daleką i długą,
tasak do mięsa, kompres i kieliszek czystej.
Dokąd tak biegnie, czy nie jest zmęczona.
Ależ nie, tylko trochę, bardzo, nic nie szkodzi.
Albo go kocha, albo się uparła.
Na dobre, na niedobre i na litość boską.

Wisława Szymborska

When he stops looking at me
I search for my reflection
on a wall. And I see only
a nail from which a picture
has been removed.

Wislawa Szymborska
translated by *Grazýna* Drabik and *Sharon Olds*

THE WOMAN'S PORTRAIT

Must be open to choices.
Changing, only let nothing be changed.
It's easy, impossible, difficult, worth trying.
She has eyes, if necessary, now cerulean blue, now grey,
black, merry, for no reason full of tears.
She sleeps with him like the first in line, the only one
                                    in the world.
She will bear him four children, no children, one.
Naive, but she'll give the best advice.
Weak, but she'll manage.
Does not have a good head on her shoulders, so she will have one.
She reads Jaspers and women's magazines.
Does not know what this bolt is for, but will build a bridge.
Young, ever young, still young.
She holds in her hands a little sparrow with a broken wing,
her own money for a long journey,
a meat chopper, a compress and a glass of vodka.
Where is she running like that, isn't she tired.
Oh no, only a little bit, very, it doesn't matter.
She either loves him, or has just set her mind.
For good, for bad and for goodness' sake.

Wislawa Szymborska
translated by *Grazýna* Drabik and *Sharon Olds*

SONNET XVI

Apres qu'un tems la gresle et le tonnerre
Ont le haut mont de Caucase batu,
Le beau iour vient, de lueur reuétu.
Quand Phebus ha son cerne fait en terre,

Et l'Ocean il regaigne à grand erre:
Sa seur se montre auec son chef pointu.
Quand quelque tems le Parthe ha combatu,
Il prent la fuite et son arc il desserre.

Un tems t'ay vu et consolé pleintif,
Et defiant de mon feu peu hatif:
Mais maintenant que tu m' as embrassee,

Et suis au point auquel tu me voulois,
Tu as ta flame en quelque eau arrosee,
Et es plus froit qu'estre ie ne soulois.

Louise Labé

SONNET XVI

Summers we'd walk this coast for hours,
come back spilling shells,
the sand enameled w/mother of pearl.

I brought peaches to take the bitter words from yr. mouth.
I kept my lamp low then.

And you came in from Oregon, hungry for light,
turning up all the wicks
till I split w/heat
like rocks at the edge of a beach fire.

> After the hail and thunder,
> the bands of color.
> After the tide goes out, anemones
> and the barnacles' ghost talk.
> After the sun, the moon.

> Only your changes ring cold.

> Cold as this midwinter beach
> where there are no shells,
> the waves beat in too strong,
> leave only the lines of their own body
> in shattered coral and sand.

> My bones breaking under yr. kiss,
> a pattern of crystal and pearled ivory,
> taking the shape of you, ringed w/frost.

Louise Labé
translated by *Sybil James*

Note: These free translations, or translitics, follow the Ezra Pound philosophy of translation where the emphasis falls, not on close rendering, but on recreating the feeling of the original, especially the poet's voice. I have kept the themes and the voice, while changing the form and using imagery that echoes the original. S.J.

BUFFALOES

The young widow
thinks she should have burned on
her husband's funeral pyre.
She could not, for her mother-in-law
insisted she raise the only son
of her only son.
The young widow sits outside
in the garden overlooking a large pond —
out of the way, still untouchable, she suckles
her three week old son
and thinks she could live
for those hungry lips, live to let him grow
bigger than herself . . . her dreams lie
lazily swishing their tails
in her mind like buffaloes
dozing — some with only nostrils showing
in a muddy pond . . .

tails switch
to keep fat flies away,
and horns, as long as a man's hand, or longer
keep the boys, and their pranks away.
It is to the old farmer's tallest son
they give their warm yellowish milk —
he alone approaches: dark-skinned and naked
except for a white turban, a white loincloth . . .
He joins them in the pond
greets each one with love:
"my beauty," "my pet" —
slaps water on their broad flanks
splashes more water on their dusty backs —
ears get scratched, necks rubbed,
drowsy faces are splashed awake —
Now he prods them out of the mud
out of the water, begging loudly
"come my beauty, come my pet, let us go!"
and the pond shrinks back
as the wide black buffaloes rise . . .

The young widow
roams from tree to tree,
newly opened leaves brush damp sweet smells
across her face . . . the infant's mouth sleeps
against her breast — dreams stuck
inside her chest twitch
as she watches the buffaloes pass
too close to her house, up the steep road
to the dairy — the loud loving voice
of the farmer's son holds them steady
without the bite of any stick or whip.

Sujata P. Bhatt

הַזֶּמֶר אֶל יַעֲקֹב שֶׁהֶאֱבַן מֵעַל פִּי הַבְּאֵר הֵסִיט

הוּא לֹא יָדַע שֶׁאֲנִי לֵאָה

וַאֲנִי — לֵאָה הָיִיתִי.

רָחֵל, אָמַר, רָחֵל, כְּכַבְשָׂה שֶׁהֶעָשָׁב מִתְעָרֶה בָּהּ

כָּךְ עֲרוּיִים בָּךְ גִּבְעוֹלִים.

עֶדְרֵי רְחֵלִים הֵמוּ בֵּין שְׁמִיכוֹתֵינוּ,

יְרִיעוֹת הָאֹהֶל נִמְשְׁכוּ אֶל הָרוּחַ.

רָחֵל, אָמַר, רָחֵל —

וְעֵינַי רָפוֹת הָיוּ

כְּקַרְקָעִית שֶׁל בִּיצָה אֲפֵלָה.

אַל חַלְּבוֹנִי עֵינַי לִבְנֵי עֵינָיו הִתְּכוּ.

יִתְרֵי הָאֹהֶל הִתְאַמְּצוּ כָּל כָּךְ

אֶל הָאֲדָמָה לִדְבֹּק

כְּשֶׁהָרוּחַ מְפַפּוֹת יָדַי נוֹשֶׁבֶת.

וְהוּא לֹא יָדַע שֶׁלֵּאָה אֲנִי

וְעֶדְרֵי בָּנִים פָּרְצוּ מֵרַחֲמִי אֶל יָדָיו.

רִבְקָה מִרְיָם

THE TUNE TO JACOB WHO THE STONE
FROM THE MOUTH OF THE WELL MOVED

He didn't know I was Leah
and I — I was Leah.
Rachel, he said, Rachel, like a lamb
the grass becomes part of, stems are a part of you.
Flocks of sheep hummed between our blankets,
tent-flies were pulled to the wind.
Rachel, he said, Rachel —
and my eyes, they were weak
the bottom of a dark swamp.
The whites of his eyes melted
to the whites of my eyes.
The cords of his tent held fast to the ground
while the wind was blowing from the palms of my hands.

And he didn't know I was Leah
and flocks of sons broke through my womb to his hands.

Rivka Miriam
translated by *Linda Zisquit*

AMOR

Sólo la voz, la piel, la superficie
pulida de las cosas.

Basta. No quiero más la oreja, que su cuenco
rebalsaría y la mano ya no alcanza
a tocar más allá.
Distraída, resbala, acariciando
y lentamente sabe del contorno.
Se retira saciada,
sin advertir el ulular inútil
de la cautividad de las entrañas
ni el impetu del cuajo de la sangre
que embiste la compuerta del borbotón, ni el nudo
ya para siempre ciego del sollozo.

El que se va se lleva su memoria,
su modo de ser río, de ser aire,
de ser adiós y nunca.

Hasta que un día otro lo para, lo detiene
y lo reduce a voz, a piel, a superficie
ofrecida, entregada, mientras dentro de sí
la oculta soledad aguarda y tiembla.

Rosario Castellanos

RETORNO

Has muerto tantas veces; nos hemos despedido
en cada muelle,
en cada andén de los desgarramientos,
amor mío, y regresas
con otro faz de flor recién abierta
que no te reconozco hasta que palpo
dentro de mí la antigua cicatriz
en la que deletreo arduamente tu nombre.

Rosario Castellanos

66

LOVE

Only the voice, the skin, the polished
surface of things.

Enough. The ear wants no more, for its bowl
would brim over and the hand reaches
no farther now to touch.
Absently it slips, stroking,
and slowly it knows the contour.
Sated, it withdraws,
not noticing the futile howl
of the entrails in captivity
nor the blood's push to coagulate
that attacks the sluicegate of the flood, nor the knot,
already blind forever, of the sob.

He who goes off takes his memory,
his way of being river, being air,
farewell and never.

Until one day someone stops, detains,
reduces him to voice, to skin, to offered
surrendered surface, while within him
the hidden solitude bides its time and trembles.

Rosario Castellanos
translated by *Carolyne Wright*

RETURN

You've died so many times; we've said goodbye
on every pier,
on every platform of laceration,
my love, and you come back
with another face of a flower recently opened
so that I don't recognize you until I touch
within myself the ancient scar
on which I spell out painstakingly your name.

Rosario Castellanos
translated by *Carolyne Wright*

CASI EL VERANO

Yo no digo que el sol, inaprehensible sueño de mi piel
entabla una demanda amorosa contra el latido del día.
Digo solamente que mi amor es un gajo desnudo
que se cubre con hojas de ruibarbo y jazmines embotellados.
Mi amore está desnudo y ha empezado a tatuar corazones en
    el viento,
iconoclastas corazones dispensadores de azules albas.

Nunca la música ha cabalgado en potros más esbeltos.
Los antiguos pavorreales del verano han empezado
a mirarse desplegando sus arpas de colores.

A la luz del verano, salta, canta, corazón.
El aire quiere dormirse junto a tu boca.
Tu corazón es una maquinaria secreta que me traga.
La lluvia nos conduce de la mano hasta el pan tierno de su abrazo.
A sus puertas estamos. Sobrecogidos y aromados.

La mañana no quiere parecerse a ninguna.
En el viento cercano una palabra tiembla.
La niña ciega alcanza el sueño de la abeja.
En tanto que nosotros transcurrimos.

Thelma Nava

ALMOST SUMMER

I do not say that the sun, inapprehensible dream of my flesh,
files the amorous petition against the day's dying,
I say only that love is a blind branch
that covers itself with rhubarb leaves and bottled jasmine.
My love, naked, embroiders hearts in the wind,
iconoclastic hearts bleeding into dawn.

Never has music ridden on more slender horses.
Summer's antique peacocks display their colorful harps.

Heart, leap and sing to summer's light.
The air yearns to sleep next to your mouth.
Your heart is a machine that swallows me.
Rain carries us by hand to the green field of your embrace.
We are at your door, startled, perfumed.

Morning does not want to appear to anyone.
In the circling wind a tear shivers.
The blind girl catches hold of the bee's dream.
We pass through time.

Thelma Nava
translated by *Nancy Prothro*

POIDS D'ANGOISSE

La terre s'ouvre sous mon poids d'angoisse
elle tremble sous moi elle a montré
son ventre rugissant et sa nuit noire
et je vois s'enliser les peupliers
Je ne puis supporter que la lumière
s'éteigne et m'abandonne à mourir
qu'elle ne lacère plus le chemin
qu'elle ne distingue plus la maison
où j'avais des fleurs où j'avais des chambres
des cerceaux d'enfants suspendus partout
des seaux qui grinçaient remplis d'eaux de pluie
J'écoute battre en moi un coeur étrange
qui me frappe au coeur mille fois trop fort
toute chair chancelle et l'âme elle-même
est ce ravin fou qui gronde et qui roule
dans le sein des fleuves déspérés

Vous aviez un nom, même votre songe
traçait des anneaux des dessins parfaits
des cris familiers jaillissaient du monde
et vous habitiez le temps des mourons
La terre sous moi se creuse une tombe
– ses effrois géants brisent le silence –
vous chasse à longs cris, cède sous vos pas
elle vous reprend au fond de son ventre
vous berce et vous tord, vous arrache à l'herbe
aux hortensias aux pluies et aux femmes
au sommeil léger des veilles l'automne
quand on craint pour soi les voleurs de pommes
La terre trahit les noms et les formes
vous changez de chair et tournerez cendres
sans m'avoir laissé le temps d'oublier
la face inconnue qu'elle et vous trompiez.

Suzanne Paradis

ANGUISH

The earth opens under my anguish
she trembles under me she has shown
her roaring belly and her black night
and I see the poplars sucked down
I cannot bear the light
extinguished and abandoning me for dead
no longer slashing the road
no longer marking the house
where I had flowers where I had rooms
children's hoops suspended everywhere
creaking pails filled with rainwater
I hear a strange heart beat within me
striking my heart a thousand times too hard
flesh staggers and the soul
is this crazy ravine scolding and rolling
in the bosom of desperate rivers

You had a name, even your dream
traced rings of perfect designs
familiar cries sprang from the world
and you lived in the time of the pimpernel.
The earth under me hollows a tomb
— her giant fright breaks the silence —
chases you with long cries, gives way under your step
she takes you up into the bottom of her belly
cradles you and twists you, snatches you from the grass
hydrangeas rains and women
light sleep of autumn vigil
when we are afraid of apple thieves
The earth betrays names and shapes
you change flesh and turn to ashes
without having left me the time to forget
the unknown face that she and you deceived.

Suzanne Paradis
translated by *Maryann De Julio*

Сжала руки под темной вуалью . . .
«Отчего ты сегодня бледна?»
— Оттого, что я терпкой печалью
Напоила его допьяна.

Как забуду? Он вышел, шатаясь,
Искривился мучительно рот . . .
Я сбежала, перил не касаясь,
Я бежала за ним до ворот.

Задыхаясь, я крикнула: «Шутка
Все, что было. Уйдешь, я умру».
Улыбнулся спокойно и жутко
И сказал мне: «Не стой на ветру».

Анна Ахматова   1911, Киев

Память о солнце в сердце слабеет.
Желтей трава.
Ветер снежинками ранними веет
Едва-едва.

В узких каналах уже не струится —
Стынет вода.
Здесь никогда ничего не случится, —
О, никогда!

Ива на небе пустом распластала
Веер сквозной.
Может быть лучше, что я не стала
Вашей женой.

Память о солнце в сердце слабеет.
Что это? — Тьма?
Может быть! За ночь прийти успеет
Зима.

Анна Ахматова   1911, Киев

72

Under her dark veil she clenched her hands . . .
"Why are you so pale today?"
"Because I made him drink harsh grief
Until he got drunk on it.

How can I forget? He staggered out,
His mouth twisted in pain . . .
I flew down the stairs after him
And caught up with him at the gate.

Panting, I cried: 'It was only a joke!
If you leave me, I'll die.'
His smile was so terrible, so calm,
And he said: 'Don't stand here in the wind.'"

Anna Akhmatova   *1911 Kiev*
translated by *Judith Hemschemeyer* and *Anna Wilkinson*

The heart's memory of the sun grows faint,
The grass is sere.
A few early snowflakes blow in the wind,
Barely, barely.

The water chills in the narrow canals,
No longer flowing.
Nothing will ever happen here —
Ah, never!

The willow spreads its lacy fan
Against an empty sky.
Perhaps it's better I didn't become
Your wife.

The heart's memory of the sun grows faint.
What's this? Darkness?
It could be. And during the night
Winter will have time to come.

Anna Akhmatova   *1911 Kiev*
translated by *Judith Hemschemeyer* and *Anna Wilkinson*

ВЕЧЕРОМ

Звенела музыка в саду
Таким невыразимым горем.
Свежо и остро пахли морем
На блюде устрицы во льду.

Он мне сказал: «Я верный друг!»
И моего коснулся платья.
Как не похожи на объятья
Прикосновенья этих рук.

Так гладят кошек или птиц,
Так на наездниц смотрят стройных.
Лишь смех в глазах его спокойных
Под легким золотом ресниц.

А скорбных скрипок голоса
Поют за стелющимся дымом:
«Благослови же небеса —
Ты первый раз одна с любимым».

Анна Ахматова   1913, Март

IN THE EVENING

The music rang out in the garden
With such inexpressible grief.
Oysters in ice on the plate
Smelled fresh and sharp, of the sea.

He told me: "I am a true friend!"
And touched my dress.
How unlike a caress,
The touch of those hands.

As one might stroke a cat or a bird,
Or watch a slender equestrienne ride . . .
Under the light gold lashes
There is only laughter in his tranquil eyes.

And the voices of mournful violins
Sing from behind the drifting smoke:
"Praise heaven! For the first time
You are with your beloved alone."

Anna Akhmatova   *March 1913*
translated by *Judith Hemschemeyer* and *Anna Wilkinson*

Как соломинкой пьешь мою душу.
Знаю, вкус ее горек и хмелен.
Но я пытку мольбой не нарушу.
О, покой мой многонеделен.

Когда кончишь, скажи. Не печально,
Что души моей нет на свете.
Я пойду дорогой недальней
Посмотреть, как играют дети.

На кустах зацветает крыжовник,
И везут кирпичи за оградой.
Кто ты: брат мой или любовник,
Я не помню, и помнить не надо.

Как светло здесь и как бесприютно,
Отдыхает усталое тело . . .
А прохожие думают смутно:
Верно, только вчера овдовела.

Анна Ахматова   1911,
                        Царское Село

As if with a straw you drink my soul.
I know it's a heady and bitter taste.
But I won't plead to end the torment;
I've been at peace for weeks and weeks.

Let me know when you're done.
It's not sad that my soul is gone.
I'll just walk down that nearby road
And watch the children play.

The gooseberry bushes are blooming;
They're hauling bricks behind the fence.
Brother or lover — who are you?
I don't remember and I don't have to.

It's so light here, so unsheltered.
My tired body rests . . .
And passers-by are thinking, vague,
"Why, she was widowed just yesterday . . ."

Anna Akhmatova   *1911 Tsarkoye Selo*
translated by *Judith Hemschemeyer* and *Anna Wilkinson*

卜算子　寫梅寄外時在粤東　董琬貞

折得嶺頭梅，憶着江南雪。君到江南雪一鞭，可是梅時節。　畫得一枝成，沒個人評閱，抵得家書寄與看，瘦似人今日。

calligraphy by Yang Toa-Ping

78

I PAINT PLUM BLOSSOMS FOR MY HUSBAND WHILE I AM LIVING IN EASTERN KUANGTUNG PROVINCE WHERE PLUMS BLOSSOM FIRST
Tz'u to the tune of P'u Suan Tzu "Fortune Telling"

I broke a plum twig on the Hill
Thinking of the Kiangnan snow.
When you got to Kiangnan,
    your whip was snow.
Is it plum season there yet?

I finished a painting of the twig
But there was no one to look it over.
As a pledge of a letter,
    I send it for you to read.
The twig is as thin as I am now.

Tung Wan-cheng
translated by *Li Chi* and *Michael O'Connor*

La Novia que se espanta de ver la vida abierta *oil on canvas 63 x 81.5 cm.* Frida Kahlo

collection of Mr. and Mrs. Jacques Gelman

Autorretrato como tehuana   *oil on masonite 24¾" x 24"*   **Frida Kahlo**

collection of Mr. and Mrs. Jacques Gelman

Autorretrato con mono   *oil on canvas 23¼" x 16½"*   **Frida Kahlo**

collection of Robert Brady

Frida y la Cesarea   *oil on canvas .73 x .62 cm*   Frida Kahlo

collection of Museo Frida Kahlo

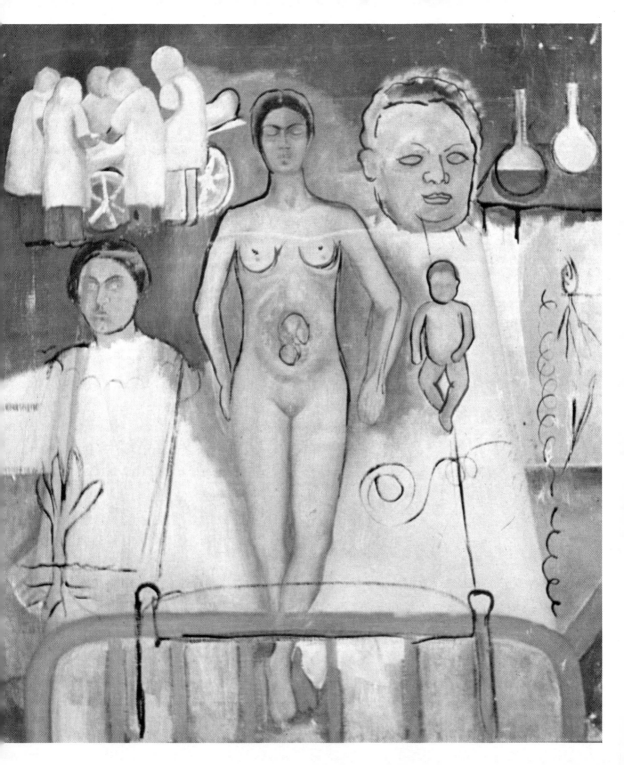

PREFACE

Frida Kahlo (1910-1954) was a visually potent artist who lived and worked in the very large shadow of her famous husband, Diego Rivera (1886-1957). Changing aesthetics and a wave of feminist art historians have begun to slowly shift the shadows, but Kahlo's prolific husband is still the better-known of the two Mexican painters.

Their work is not similar. Rivera covered huge walls, both in Mexico and the United States, with beautifully painted and often blatantly political murals. He was one of the founding fathers of the Mexican mural movement. From 1922 onward his brush swept panoramas of Mexican history across walls in the true fresco technique. His murals glorified the Mexican Revolution, Mexico's Indian heritage, and the humble peasant. Although he was expelled from the Communist party in 1929, his murals, which were painted for the worker, continued to fit snugly into Communist ideas on art at that time.

Kahlo, on the other hand, painted a series of small self-portraits of an unusually intimate nature. All of her dramatic life was recorded in her paintings: her miscarriages, the emotional ups and downs of her love life, and the recurring physical problems brought on by a traffic accident in her youth. Though Kahlo was also a Communist, her paintings did not conform to Communist theories about painting. In fact, if carefully analyzed, her images would have been considered heretical.

Portrait of Diego is essentially the work of a proud wife praising her husband. It is interesting precisely because the wife was as substantial an artist and intellect as the subject. The political rhetoric in the essay seems dated, but Kahlo's feelings about subjects ranging from jealousy to her pride in her husband's collection of pre-Columbian art are fascinating. *Portrait of Diego* illuminates a marriage that was simultaneously difficult and passionate, draining and nourishing.

Kahlo subordinated her needs and her career to Rivera. In spite of this, the content and the style of her work stands firm in its individuality while scores of male artists of her generation fell into glib imitation of Rivera. A quarter century after her death, Frida Kahlo's paintings are increasingly pertinent and fresh.

Nancy Breslow
Chicago, September 11, 1980

I would like to express my deep gratitude to Fernando Gamboa, the director of the Museo de Arte Moderno in Mexico City, who originally advised me to translate this essay. Special thanks also go to Babara Vondrak and Joan Collett who made valuable suggestions during the later stages of the evolution of this translation. N.B.

Verde: luz tibia y buena.

Solferino: Azteca tlapalli. Vieja sangre de tuna. El más vivo y antiguo.

Café: color de mole, de hoja que se va. Tierra.

Amarillo: locura, enfermedad, miedo. Parte del sol y de la alegría.

Azul cobalto: electricidad y pureza. Amor.

Negro: nada es negro, realmente nada.

Verde hoja: hojas, tristeza, ciencia. Alemania entera es de este color.

Amarillo verdoso: más locura y misterio. Todos los fantasmas usan trajes
    de este color...o cuando
    menos ropa interior.

Verde oscuro: color de anuncios malos y de buenos negocios.

Azul marino: distancia. También la ternura puede ser de este azul.

Magenta: ¿sangre? Pues ¡quién sabe!

Frida Kahlo

Green: tepid and good light

Reddish-purple: Azteca Tlapalli. Old blood of the prickly pear.
                    The most alive and ancient.

Brown: color of *mole,* of the falling leaf. Earth.

Yellow: insanity, sickness, fear. Part of the sun and of joy.

Cobalt blue: electricity and purity. Love.

Black: nothing is black, really nothing.

Leaf Green: leaves, sadness, science. All of Germany is this color.

Greenish yellow: more insanity and mystery. All the ghosts wear clothes this
                     color . . . or at least underwear.

Dark green: color of bad advertisements and good business deals.

Navy blue: distance. Also tenderness could be this blue.

Magenta: blood? Well, who knows!

Frida Kahlo (from her diary)
translated by *Julietta Ackerman*

RETRATO DE DIEGO

Advierto que este retrato de Diego lo pintaré con colores que no conozco: las palabras, y por ésto, será pobre; además, quiero en tal forma a Diego que no puedo ser "espectadora" de su vida, sino parte, por lo que – quizá – exageraré lo positivo de su personalidad única tratando de desvanecer lo que, aun remotamente, puede herirlo. No será esto un relato biográfico: considero más sincero escribir solamente sobre el Diego que yo creo haber conocido un poco en estos veinte años que he vivido cerca de él. No hablaré de Diego como de "mi esposo," porque sería ridículo; Diego no ha sido jamás ni será "esposo" de nadie. Tampoco como de un amante, porque él abarca mucho más allá de las limitaciones sexuales, y si hablara de él como de un hijo, no haría sino describir o pintar mi propia emoción, casi mi autorretrato, no el de Diego. Con esta advertencia, y con toda limpieza, trataré de decir la única verdad: la mía, que esboce, dentro de mi capacidad, su imagen.

Su forma: Con su cabeza asiática sobre la que nace un pelo obscuro, tan delgado y fino que parece flotar en el aire, Diego es un niño grandote, inmenso, de cara amable y mirada un poco triste. Sus ojos saltones, obscuros, inteligentísimos y grandes, están difícilmente detenidos – casi fuera de las órbitas – por párpados hinchados y protuberantes como de batracio, muy separados uno del otro, más que otros ojos. Sirven para que su mirada abarque un campo visual mucho más amplio, como si estuvieran construidos especialmente para un pintor de los espacios y las multitudes. Entre esos ojos, tan distantes uno de otro, se adivina lo invisible de la sabiduría oriental, y muy pocas veces, desaparece de su boca búdica, de labios carnosos, una sonrisa irónica y tierna, flor de su imagen.

Viéndolo desnudo, se piensa inmediatamente en un niño rana, parado sobre las patas de atrás. Su piel es blanco-verdosa, como de animal acuático. Solamente sus manos y su cara son más obscuras, porque el sol las quemó.

Sus hombros infantiles, angostos y redondos, se continúan sin ángulos en brazos femeninos, terminando en unas manos maravillosas, pequeñas y de fino dibujo, sensibles y sutiles como antenas que comunican con el universo entero. Es asombroso que esas manos hayan servido para pintar tanto y trabajen todavía infatigablemente.

De su pecho hay que decir que: si hubiera desembarcado en la isla que gobernaba Safo, no hubiera sido ejecutado por sus guerreras. La sensibilidad de sus maravillosos senos lo habieran hecho admisible. Aunque su virilidad, específica y extraña, lo hace deseable también en dominios de emperatrices ávidas del amor masculino.

Su vientre, enorme, terso y tierno como una esfera, descansa sobre sus fuertes piernas, bellas como columnas, que rematan en grandes pies, los cuales se abren

PORTRAIT OF DIEGO

I warn you that I shall paint this portrait of Diego with colors that are unfamiliar to me: words, and for this reason, it will be poor. Moreover, I love Diego in a way that means I can't be a "spectator" to his life, but a part of it, for which reason — perhaps — I will exaggerate the positive aspects of his unique personality trying to remove that which, even remotely, could hurt him. It will not be a biographic statement; I consider it more sincere to write only about the Diego that I believe I have known a little in these twenty years that I have lived near him. I will not speak of Diego as "my husband" because it would be ridiculous; Diego never has been nor ever will be "husband" to anyone. Nor as a lover, because he embraces much more than the sexual limitations; and if I will speak of him as of a son, I would only describe or paint my own emotion, almost my self-portrait not that of Diego. With this warning, and with all honesty, I will try my truth: the truth, that his image sketches within my mind.

HIS FORM: With his Asiatic head above which his dark hair grows, so thin and fine that it seems to float in the air, Diego is a giant child, immense, of kind face and a slightly sad look. His bulging eyes, dark, very intelligent and huge, are constrained with difficulty — they are almost outside their orbits — because of swollen and protruding eyelids like a Bactrachian, very separate one from the other. Because of them his vision embraces a visual field much more ample, as if it were constructed especially for a painter of spaces and multitudes. Through these wide-set eyes invisible future events of Oriental wisdom can be foretold; only rarely does an ironic and tender smile disappear from his Buddha mouth of fleshy lips... a flower of his image.

Seeing him nude, one immediately thinks of a boy frog standing up on his hind legs. His skin is greenish-white, like an aquatic animal, but his hands and face are darker, because they are sunburned.

His childish shoulders, narrow and rounded, continue without angles into feminine arms, ending in wonderful hands, small and of fine design, sensitive and subtle like antennae that communicate with the entire universe. It is amazing that these hands serve to paint so much and still work tirelessly.

Of his chest one must say that if he had disembarked on the island governed by Sappho, he wouldn't be executed by her warrior women. The sensitivity of his wonderful breasts would have made him admissible. His virility, specific and strange, would also make him desirable in dominions of empresses covetous of masculine love.

His enormous belly, tender and smooth like a sphere, rests above his strong, beautiful, column-like legs that terminate in large feet. His feet open toward the outside in obtuse angles as if to take in the whole earth and sustain himself above

hacia afuera, en ángulo obtuso, como para abarcar toda la tierra y sostenerse sobre ella incontrastablemente, como a un ser antidiluviano, en el que emergiera, de la cintura para arriba, un ejemplar de humanidad futura, lejana de nosotros dos o tres mil años.

Duerme en posición fetal y durante su vigilia, se mueve con lentitud elegante, como si viviera dentro de un medio líquido. Para su sensibilidad, expresada en su movimiento, parece que el aire fuera más denso que el agua.

La forma de Diego, es la de un monstruo entrañable, al cual la abuela, Antigua Ocultadora, la materia necesaria y eterna, la madre de los hombres, y todos los dioses que éstos inventaron en su delirio, originados por el miedo y el hambre, LA MUJER, entre todas ellas –YO – quisiera siempre tenerlo en brazos como a su niño recién nacido.

Su CONTENIDO: Diego está al margen de toda relación personal, limitada y precisa. Contradictorio como todo lo que mueve a la vida es, a la vez, caricia inmensa y descarga violenta de fuerzas poderosas y únicas. Se le vive dentro, como a la semilla que la tierra atesora, y fuera, como a los paisajes. Probablemente algunos esperan de mí un retrato de Diego muy personal, "femenino," anecdótico, divertido, lleno de quejas y hasta de cierta cantidad de chismes, de esos chismes "decentes," interpretables y aprovechables según la morbosidad de los lectores. Quizá esperen oír de mí lamentos de "lo mucho que se sufre" viviendo con un hombre como Diego. Pero yo no creo que las márgenes de un río sufran por dejarlo correr, ni la tierra sufra porque llueva, ni el átomo sufra descargando su energía …para mí, todo tiene una compensación natural. Dentro de mi papel, difícil y obscuro, de aliada de un ser extraordinario, tengo la recompensa que tiene un punto verde dentro de una cantidad de rojo: recompensa de *equilibrio*. Las penas o alegrías que norman la vida en esta sociedad, podrida de mentiras, en la que vivo, no son las mías. Si tengo prejuicios y me hieren las acciones de los demás, aún las de Diego Rivera, me hago responsable de mi incapacidad para ver con claridad, y si no los tengo, debo admitir que es natural que los glóbulos rojos luchen contra los blancos sin el menor prejuicio y que ese fenómeno solamente signifique salud.

No seré yo quien desvalorice la fantástica personalidad de Diego, al que respeto profundamente, diciendo sobre su vida estupideces. Quisiera, por el contrario, expresar como se merece, con la poesía que no poseo, lo que Diego es en realidad.

De su pintura habla ya - prodigiosamente - su pintura misma.

De su función como organismo humano se encargarán los hombres de ciencia. De su valiosa cooperación social revolucionaria, su obra objetiva y personal, todos aquellos que sepan medir su trascendencia incalculable en el tiempo; pero yo, que le he visto vivir veinte años, no tengo medios para organizar y describir las imágenes

it insurmountably, like an antediluvian being who would emerge from the water as an example for future humanity.

He sleeps in a fetal position. During his wakefulness, he moves with slow elegance, as if living inside a liquid medium. His movement expresses his sensitivity, making air seem denser than water.

The form of Diego is that of an affectionate monster, inspired by fear and hunger, created by the ancient concealer, a necessary and eternal element, the primal mother of men and all the gods that man invented in his delirium. WOMAN, among all of them — I — would always want to cradle him like a newborn child.

HIS CONTENT: Diego is marginal in all personal relations, limited and precise. Contradictory like all that moves life, he is, at the same time, an immense caress and a violent discharge of powerful and unique forces. On the inside he is like a seed that the earth treasures, and on the outside he is like the landscape. Some may hope from me a portrait of Diego that is personal, "feminine," anecdotal, amusing, full of complaints with a certain quantity of "decent" gossip, useful to the morbidly curious. Perhaps they hope to hear my laments of "how much one suffers" living with a man like Diego. But I cannot believe that the banks of a river are damaged by allowing it to run, nor the earth is damaged by the rain, nor the atom diminished by discharging its energy…for me, all has a natural compensation. In my role, difficult and dark, as ally of an extraordinary being, I have the reward that a green point has within a great amount of red: the reward of *balance.* The pains or joys that normalize life in this society are rotted with lies, but they are not mine. If I have prejudices and the actions of others wound me, even those of Diego Rivera, I am responsible for my inability to see with clarity. If I don't have these prejudices, I ought to admit that it is natural that the red globules struggle against the white and that this phenomenon only signifies health.

It will not be I who depreciates the fantastic personality of Diego, who I profoundly respect, saying stupidities about his life. On the contrary, I would love to express with the poetry that he deserves, but which I don't possess, that which in reality is Diego.

About his painting he has already spoken — prodigiously — in his own painting.

About his function as a human organism, men of science should speak to that. About his valuable work as a social revolutionary, his objective and personal work, all those that know how to measure the magnitude of his incalculable importance will do so in time. But I, who have seen him live for twenty years, don't have the means to describe the lively profound images that, weak as they might be, at least represent the most elemental characteristics of his personality. From my heavi-

vivas que, aunque fuera débilmente, pero con hondura, dibujaran siquiera lo más elemental de su figura. Desde mi torpeza, saldrán solamente unas cuantas opiniones y serán el único material que pueda ofrecer.

Las raíces profundas, las influencias externas y las verdaderas causas que condicionan la personalidad inigualable de Diego, son tan vastas y complejas que mis observaciones serán pequeños brotes en las múltiples ramas del árbol gigantesco que es Diego.

Son tres la direcciones o líneas principales que yo considero básicas en su retrato: la primera, la de ser un luchador revolucionario constante, dinámico, extraordinariamente sensible y vital; trabajador infatigable en su oficio, que conoce como pocos pintores en el mundo; entusiasta fantástico de la vida y, a la vez, descontento siempre de no haber logrado saber más, construir más y pintar más. La segunda: la de ser un curioso eterno, investigador incansable de todo, y la tercera: su carencia absoluta de prejuicios y, por tanto, de fe, porque Diego acepta – como Montaigne – que "allí donde termina la duda comienza la estupidez" y, aquel que tiene fe en algo admite la sumisión incondicional, sin libertad de analizar o de variar el curso de los hechos. Por este clarísimo concepto de la realidad, Diego es rebelde y, conociendo maravillosamente la dialéctica materialista de la vida, Diego es revolucionario. De este triángulo, sobre el que se elaboran las demás modalidades de Diego, se desprende una especie de atmósfera que envuelve al total. Esta atmósfera móvil es el amor, pero el amor como estructura general, como movimiento constructor de belleza. Yo me imagino que el mundo que él quisiera vivir, sería una gran fiesta, en la que todos y cada uno de los seres tomara parte, desde los hombres hasta las piedras, los soles y las sombras: todos cooperando con su propia belleza y su poder creador. Una fiesta de la forma, del color, del movimiento, del sonido, de la inteligencia, del conocimiento, de la emoción. Una fiesta esférica, inteligente y amorosa, que cubriera la superficie entera de la tierra. Para hacer esa fiesta, lucha continuamente y ofrece todo cuanto tiene: su genio, su imaginación, sus palabras y sus acciones. Lucha, cada instante, por borrar en el hombre, el miedo y la estupidez.

Por su deseo profundo de ayudar a transformar la sociedad en que vive en una más bella, más sana, menos dolorosa y más inteligente, y por poner al servicio de esa Revolución Social, ineludible y positiva, toda su fuerza creadora, su genio constructor, su sensibilidad penetrante y su trabajo constante, a Diego se le ataca continuamente. Durante estos veinte años, lo he visto luchar contra el complicadísimo engranaje de las fuerzas negativas contrarias a su empuje de libertad y transformación. Vive en un mundo hostil porque el enemigo es mayoría, pero esto no lo acobarda, y mientras viva, saldrán siempre de sus manos, de sus labios y de

ness, only a few opinions will come out and they will be the only material that I can offer.

The profound roots, the external influences and the true causes that determine the unique personality of Diego, are so vast and complex that my observations will be small buds on the gigantic tree that is Diego.

There are three principle lines that I consider basic to his portrait: *First,* he is a constant revolutionary struggler: he is dynamic, extraordinarily sensitive and vital. He is an untiring worker in his craft, which he knows like few painters in his world; and he is always dissatisfied not to know more, to build more and to paint more. *Second,* he is eternally curious, and an untiring investigator of everything. *Third,* he absolutely lacks prejudice and, therefore, faith, because Diego accepts — like Montaigne — that "Stupidity begins where doubt ends." He who has faith admits to unconditional submission, without liberty to analyze or to vary the course of events. Because of his clear concept of reality, Diego is rebellious and knows marvelously the materialistic dialectic of life. Diego is revolutionary. Around this triangle, an enveloping atmosphere exists. This mobile atmosphere is of love, love as foundation of vital beauty.

I imagine that the world where he would like to live, would be a great fiesta, in which all beings would take part, from men to rocks, from suns to shadows. It would be a fiesta of form, of color, of movement, of sound, of intelligence, of knowledge, of emotion. His earth would be an intelligent and loving spherical fiesta. In order to achieve this fiesta, he continually struggles and offers all that he has: his genius, his imagination, his words and his actions. Each instant he struggles to erase fear and stupidity in man.

Diego is attacked continually because of his profound desire to help transform the society in which we live to one more fair, more sane, less painful and more intelligent. He puts all his creative force into this inevitable Social Revolution. During these twenty years, I have seen him struggle against complicated negative forces contrary to his example of liberty and transformation. Because the enemy is the majority, he lives in a hostile world, but this doesn't intimidate him. As long as he lives there will emanate from his hands, his lips and all his being the fresh combative breadth of life.

Like Diego, all those who brought light to the lands have struggled. Like them, Diego doesn't have "friends," but allies. Those alies that emerge from within himself are magnificent: his brilliant intelligence, his clear knowledge of the human material inside which he works, his great culture not of books, but inductive and deductive, and his desire to construct a world free from cowardice and lies. In our society all of us are his allies who realize the necessity of destroying the false bases of the actual world.

todo su ser, alientos nuevos, vivos, valientes y profundos de combate.

Como Diego, han luchado ya todos los que trajeron a la tierra una luz; como ellos, Diego no tiene "amigos," sino aliados. Los que emergen de sí mismo son magníficos; su inteligencia brillante, su conocimiento profundo y claro del material humano dentro del que trabaja, su experiencia sólida, su gran cultura no de libros, sino inductiva y deductiva; su genio y su deseo de construir, con cimientos de realidad, un mundo limpio de cobardía y de mentira. En la sociedad en que vive, somos sus aliados todos los que, como él, nos damos cuenta de la necesidad imperativa de destruir las bases falsas del mundo actual.

Contra los ataques cobardes que se le hacen, Diego reacciona siempre con firmeza y con un gran sentido de humor. Nunca transige ni cede: se enfrenta abiertamente a sus enemigos, solapados la mayoría y valerosos algunos, contando siempre con la realidad, nunca con elementos de "ilusión" o de "ideal." Esta intransigencia y rebeldía son fundamentales en Diego; complementan su retrato.

Entre las muchas cosas que se dicen de Diego estas son las más comunes: le llaman mitómano, buscador de publicidad y, las más ridícula, millonario. Su pretendida mitomanía está en relación directa con su tremenda imaginación, es decir, es tan mentiroso como los poetas o como los niños a los que todavía no han idiotizado la escuela o sus mamás. Yo le he oído decir toda clase de mentiras; desde las más inocentes, hasta las historias más complicadas de personajes a quienes su imaginación combina en situaciones y procederes fantásticos, siempre con gran sentido de humor y crítica maravillosa; pero nunca le he oído decir una sola mentira estúpida o banal. Mintiendo, o jugando a mentir, desenmascara a muchos, aprende el mecanismo interior de otros, mucho más ingenuamente mentirosos que él y lo más curioso de las supuestas mentiras de Diego es que, a la larga o a la corta, los involucrados en la combinación imaginaria se enojan, no por la mentira, sino por la verdad contenida en la mentira, que siempre sale a flote. Es entonces cuando se "alborota el gallinero," pues se ven descubiertos en el terreno en que precisamente se creían más protegidos. Lo que en realidad sucede es que Diego es de los muy pocos que se atreven a atacar por la base, de frente y sin miedo, a la estructura llamada MORAL de la hipócrita sociedad en que vivimos, y como la verdad no peca pero incomoda, aquellos que se ven descubiertos en sus más recónditos móviles secretos, no pueden sino llamar a Diego mentiroso, o cuando menos, exagerado.

Dicen que busca publicidad. Yo he observado que más bien tratan de hacerla los otros con él, para sus propios intereses, sólo que lo hacen con métodos jesuitas mal aplicados, porque generalmente les sale "el tiro por la culata." Diego no necesita publicidad, y mucho menos, la que en su propio país se la obsequia. Su trabajo habla por sí mismo. No solamente por lo que ha hecho en la tierra de México,

Against cowardly attacks Diego always reacts with firmness and with a great sense of humor. He never concedes nor yields; he openly confronts his enemies, the majority underhanded though some brave, he always counts on reality, rather than elements of "illusion." This intransigence and rebellion are fundamental to Diego and complement his description.

Among the many things that they say about Diego, the most common are "mythomaniac," "publicity seeker" and, most ridiculous, "millionaire." His supposed mythomania is in direct relation to his tremendous imagination, which is to say, he is as much a liar as poets or children are who have not yet been stupified by school or their mothers. I have heard him say all kinds of lies from the most innocent to the most complicated. His imagination combines people in situations and fantastic conduct, always with a great sense of humor and marvelous criticism. But, I have never heard a single stupid or banal lie. Lying, or playing at lying, he exposes many. He learns the interior workings of others, who are much more ingenuously false than he. The most curious thing about the supposed lies of Diego is that persons confused in the imaginary combination eventually become angry, not for the lie, but for the truth contained in the lie that always surfaces. "The chicken coop goes up for grabs," when they see themselves uncovered in the terrain where they believed themselves to be most protected. What happens in reality is that Diego is one of the few who dare to frontally and fearlessly attack the basis of the MORAL structure of the hypocritical society in which we live. He doesn't sin, but inconveniences those that see themselves revealed in their most hidden secret motives. They can only call Diego a liar or, at least, exaggerator.

They say he looks for publicity. On the contrary, I have seen others attack him to promote themselves, only they do it with badly applied Jesuitical methods which generally come out "ass backwards." Diego doesn't need publicity, especially not the type that is offered to him in his own country. His work speaks for itself, not only the work he has done in Mexico, where he is shamelessly insulted, but in the civilized countries of the world, where he is recognized. How incredible that the lowest, most cowardly insults against Diego have been vomited in Mexico.

Not only through the press but by acts of vandalism, they try to destroy his work. "Decent" matrons use innocent umbrellas to hypo-critically scatch lines in his paintings while passing. Acids, kitchen knives, and common spit (worthy of the possessors of more saliva than brains) are used to destroy his work. On posters are written words not appropriate to a people so Catholic. Groups of "well-bred" youths stone his house and his studio destroying irreplaceable works of pre-Columbian Mexican art which form part of Diego's collection. Persons in power assigned to look after culture for the good name of the country attach "no importance" to such attacks. Alone he tries to defend, not only for himself, but for all, freedom of expression.

donde desvergonzadamente se le insulta más que en ninguna otra parte, sino en todos los países civilizados del mundo, en los que se le reconoce como uno de los hombres más importantes y geniales en el campo de la cultura. Es increíble, por cierto, que los insultos más bajos, más cobardes y más estúpidos en contra de Diego hayan sido vomitados en su propia casa: México. Por medio de la prensa, por medio de actos bárbaros y vandálicos con los que han tratado de destruir su obra, usando desde las inocentes sombrillas de las señoras "decentes," que rayan sus pinturas hipócritamente, y como de pasada, hasta ácidos y cuchillos de comedor, no olvidando el salivazo común y corriente, digno de los poseedores de tanta saliva como poco seso; por medio de letreros en las paredes de las calles en las que se escriben palabras nada adecuadas para un pueblo tan católico; por medio de grupos de jóvenes "bien educados" que apedrean su casa y su estudio destruyendo insubstituíbles obras de arte mexicano precortesiano – que forman parte de las colecciones de Diego –, los que después de hacer su "gracia" echan a correr; por medio de cartas anónimas (es inútil hablar del valor de sus remitentes) o por medio del silencio, neutral y pilatesco, de personas en el poder, encargadas de cuidar o impartir cultura para el buen nombre del país, no dándole "ninguna importancia" a tales ataques contra la obra de un hombre que con todo su genio, su esfuerzo creador, único, trata de defender, no sólo para él, sino para todos, la libertad de expresión.

Todas estas maniobras a la sombra y a la luz se hacen en nombre de la democracia, de la moralidad y de ¡Viva México! – también se usa, a veces, ¡Viva Cristo Rey! –. Toda esta publicidad que Diego no busca, ni necesita, prueba dos cosas: que el trabajo, la obra entera, la indiscutible personalidad de Diego son de tal importancia que tienen que tomarse en cuenta por aquellos a quienes él echa en cara su hipocresía y sus planes arribistas y desvergonzados; y el estado deplorable y débil de un país – semi-colonial – que permite que sucedan en 1949 cosas que solamente podrían acontecer en plena Edad Media, en la época de la Santa Inquisición o mientras imperó Hitler en el mundo.

Para reconocer al hombre, al maravilloso pintor, al luchador valiente y al revolucionario íntegro, esperan su muerte. Mientras viva habrá muchos "machos," de esos que han recibido su educación en el "paquín," que seguirán apedreando su casa, insultándolo anónimamente o por medio de la prensa de su propio país y otros, todavía más "machos," *pico de cera,* que se lavarán las manos y pasarán a la historia envueltos en la bandera de la prudencia.

Y le llaman millonario…la única verdad en esto de los millones de Diego es ésta: siendo artesano, y no proletario, posee sus útiles de producción – es decir, de

All of these maneuvers in shadow and in the open are made in the name of democracy, of morality and of "Long live Mexico!" At times, "Long live Christ the King!" is also used. All this publicity that Diego neither looks for nor needs proves two things: that Diego's entire work and personality are so important that they have to be considered by those in whose faces he throws their own hypocrisy. The treatment of Diego shows the weak state of a semi-colonial country that permits these things to happen in 1949, things appropriate to the Dark Ages, the time of the Holy Inquisition or during Hitler's reign.

The man, the marvelous painter, the valiant struggler and honest revolutionary, will not be recognized until he is dead. While he lives there will be many machos who have received their education in comic books, who will continue to stone his house, and to insult him anonymously or through the press. And they call him mil- lionaire…the only truth about Diego's millions is that being an artisan, and not proletariat, he possesses his tools of production, a house in which he lives, rags that he throws on his back, and a worn-out station wagon that serves like a tailor's scissors. His treasure is a collection of wonderful sculptured works, jewels of indigenous art, living heart of the true Mexico. With incredible economic sacrifices he has succeeded in gathering this collection over a period of more than thirty years in order to place it in a museum that he has been constructing for the last seven years. He has achieved this work with his own creative and economic efforts. He will donate it to his country, willing to Mexico the most prodigious fountain of beauty that has existed, a gift for the eyes of Mexicans who have an incalculable admiration for the outdoors.

Except for this, economically he doesn't have anything; he doesn't possess anything other than his will to work. Last year he didn't have sufficient money to get out of the hospital after he suffered from pneumonia. Still convalescent, he began painting in order to meet the daily expenses of life and the salaries of the workers who, like in the guilds of the Renaissance, cooperate with him in order to construct the marvelous Pedregal.

But insults and attacks don't change Diego. They form part of the social phenomena of a world in decadence and nothing more. All of life continues to intrigue him, enchant him with its variety, and surprise him with its beauty. Nothing disillusions him nor intimidates him.

Being an astute observer, he has achieved an experience that, united to his — I would say, interior knowledge of things — and his intense culture, permit him to delve into the causes. Like a surgeon, he opens to discover the deepest and most hidden; trying to achieve something certain, he betters the function of the organism. For this reason Diego is neither defeated nor sad. Fundamentally he is an investigator, builder, and above all, an architect. He is an architect in his

trabajo –, una casa en la que vive, trapos que echarse encima y una camioneta desvencijada que le sirve como a los sastres las tijeras. Su tesoro es una colección de obras escultóricas maravillosas, joyas del arte indígena, corazón vivo del México verdadero, que con indecibles sacrificios económicos ha logrado reunir en más de treinta años para colocarla en un museo que está construyendo desde hace siete. Esta obra la ha levantado con su propio esfuerzo creador y con su propio esfuerzo económico, es decir, con su talento maravilloso y con lo que le pagan por sus pinturas; la donará a su país, legando a México la fuente más prodigiosa de belleza que haya existido, regalo para los ojos de los mexicanos que los tengan y admiración incalculable para los de afuera. Excepto ésto, económicamente no tiene nada; no posee otra cosa que su fuerza de trabajo. El año pasado no tenía el dinero suficiente para salir del hospital, después de sufrir una pulmonía. Todavía convaleciente, se puso a pintar para sacar los gastos de la vida diaria y los salarios de los obreros que, como en los gremios del Renacimiento, cooperan con él para construir la obra maravillosa de Pedregal.

Pero a Diego los insultos y los ataques no lo cambian. Forman parte de los fenómenos sociales de un mundo en decadencia y nada más. La vida entera le sigue interesando y maravillando, por cambiante, y todo le sorprende por bello, pero nada le *decepciona* ni le acobarda porque conoce el mecanismo dialéctico de los fenómenos y de los hechos.

Observador agudísimo, ha logrado una experiencia que, unida a su conocimiento – podría yo decir, interno, de las cosas – y a su intensa cultura, le permite desentrañar las causas. Como los cirujanos, abre para ver, para descubrir lo más hondo y escondido y lograr algo cierto, positivo, que mejore las circunstancias y el funcionamiento de los organismos. Por eso Diego no es ni derrotista ni triste. Es, fundamentalmente, investigador, constructor, y sobre todo, arquitecto. Es arquitecto en su pintura, en su proceso de pensar y en el deseo apasionado de estructurar una sociedad armónica, funcional y sólida. Compone siempre con elementos precisos, matemáticos. No importa si su composición es un cuadro, una casa o un argumento. Sus cimientos son siempre la realidad. La poesía que sus obras contienen es la de los números, la de las fuentes vivas de la historia. Sus leyes, las leyes físicas y firmes que rigen la vida entera de los átomos a los soles. Prueba magnífica de su genio de arquitecto son sus murales que se ligan, viven, con la construcción misma del edificio que los contiene, con la función material y organizada de ellos.

La obra estupenda que está construyendo en el pueblo de San Pablo Tepetlapa, a la que él llama *el anahuacali* (casa de Anáhuac), destinada a guardar su inigualable colección de escultura antigua mexicana, es un enlace de formas antiguas y nuevas, creación magnífica que hará perdurar y revivir la arquitectura

painting, in his process of thinking and in his passionate desire to construct a harmonic, functional, and solid society. He always composes with precise mathematical elements. Whether he is composing a painting, a house or an argument, he builds upon reality. The poetry that his works contain is that of numbers. His laws are the physical laws that govern the whole life of atoms and suns. His murals are allied to the construction of the buildings that contain them and are magnificent proof of his architectural genius.

The stupendous work that he is constructing in the town of San Pablo Tepetlapa, which he calls *el anahuacali* (house of Anahuac), is destined to house his unequaled collection of ancient Mexican sculpture. This magnificent creation interlocks old and new forms and brings a new dimension to the architecture of Mexico. It grows in the incredibly beautiful landscape of the Pedregal like an enormous Cactaceae that looks to Ajusco, sober and elegant, ancient and perennial. It shouts, with a voice of centuries and days, from the core of the volcanic rock: "Mexico is alive!" Like Coatlicue,* it contains life and death; like the magnificent terrain in which it's founded, it hugs the earth with the firmness of a plant.

Since Diego is always working, he doesn't live a normal life. His capacity of energy breaks clocks and calendars. He generates and receives waves difficult to compare to others. His immense receptor and creator mechanisms make him insatiable. The images and the ideas flow in his brain with an uncommon rhythm and for this reason his desire to expand is uncontainable. This causes indecision. His indecision is superficial, because ultimately, he succeeds in doing whatever he wants to do with a predetermined will. Nothing paints this aspect of his character better than an anecdote his aunt Cesarita once told me. She remembered that when Diego was young he entered one of those mixed-up general stores, full of magic and surprise that we all remember with affection, and stood in front of the display case, with some centavos in his hand. He looked and looked over all the contents in the store, furiously shouting all the while: "What do I want!" The store was called "The Future," and Diego's indecision has lasted all his life. But although he rarely makes up his mind to choose, he carries inside a vector-line that goes directly to the center of his will.

Being eternally curious, he is the eternal conversationalist. He can paint hours and days without resting, chattering while working. He speaks and discusses absolutely everything. Like Walt Whitman he enjoys speaking with all who want to hear him. His conversation is always interesting. He has sentences that amaze, wound, stir up emotions, but he never leaves those who hear him with the impression of idleness or emptiness. His words disturb because they are alive and true. The rawness of his concepts enervates those who listen because they do not

*Coatlicue was the pre-Columbian goddess of earth and the mother of the gods. She was known as the "Goddess of the Serpent Skirt."

incomparable de la tierra de México. Crece en el paisaje increíblemente bello del Pedregal como una enorme cactácea que mira al Ajusco, sobria y elegante, fuerte y fina, antigua y perenne; grita, con voces de siglos y de días, desde sus entrañas de piedra volcánica: ¡México está vivo! Como la Coatlicue, contiene la vida y la muerte; como el terreno magnífico en que está erigida, se abraza a la tierra con la firmeza de una planta viva y permanente.

Trabajando siempre, Diego no vive una vida que pudiera llamarse normal. Su capacidad de energía rompe los relojes y los calendarios. Materialmente, le falta tiempo para luchar, sin descanso, proyectando y realizando constantemente su obra. Genera y recoge ondas difíciles de comparar a otras, y el resultado de su mecanismo receptor y creador, siendo tan vasto y tan inmenso, jamás lo satisface. Las imágenes y las ideas fluyen en su cerebro con un ritmo diferente a lo común y por ésto su intensidad de fijación y su deseo de hacer siempre más son incontenibles. Este mecanismo lo hace indeciso. Su indecisión es superficial, porque, finalmente, logra hacer lo que le da la gana con una voluntad segura y planeada. Nada pinta mejor esta modalidad de su carácter que aquello que una vez me contó su tía Cesarita, hermana de su madre. Recordaba que, siendo Diego muy niño, entró en una tienda, de esos tendajones mixtos llenos de magia y de sorpresa que todos recordamos con cariño, y parado frente al mostrador, con unos centavos en la mano, miraba y repasaba todo el universo contenido dentro de la tienda, mientras gritaba desesperado y furioso: ¡Qué quiero! La tienda se llamaba "El Porvenir," y esta indecisión de Diego ha durado toda su vida. Pero aunque pocas veces se decide a escoger, lleva dentro una línea-*vector* que va directamente al centro de su voluntad y su deseo.

Siendo el eterno curioso, es, a la vez, el eterno conversador. Puede pintar horas y días sin descansar, charlando mientras trabaja. Habla y discute de todo, absolutamente de todo, gozando, como Walt Whitman, con todos los que quieran oírlo. Su conversación siempre interesa. Tiene frases que asombran, que a veces hieren; otras conmueven, pero jamás deja al que lo oye con la impresión de inutilidad o de vacío. Sus palabras inquietan tremendamente por vivas y ciertas. La crudeza de sus conceptos enerva o descontrola al que lo escucha porque ninguno de éstos comulga con las normas de conducta ya establecidas; rompen siempre la corteza para dejar nacer brotes; hieren para dejar crecer nuevas células. A algunos, a los más fuertes, la conversación y el contenido de verdad de Diego les parece monstruoso, sádico, cruel; a otros, los más débiles, los anula y los anonada y la defensa de éstos consiste en llamarlo mentiroso y fantástico. Pero todos tratan de defenderse de una manera muy semejante a como se defienden contra la vacuna, los que por primera vez en su vida van a ser vacunados. Invocan a la esperanza o a algo que los libre del peligro de la verdad. Pero Diego Rivera está desprovisto de fe,

agree with the established norms of conduct; they break the bark in order to give birth to the buds; they wound in order to allow new cells to grow. To the strongest, the conversation and the truthful content of Diego seems monstrous, sadistic, cruel; to the weakest, it nullifies them and overwhelms them and their only defense is to call him liar. But all try to defend themselves in the same way that those who are vaccinated for the first time to defend themselves against the vaccine. They invoke hope to free them from the danger of the truth. But Diego Rivera is deprived of faith, hope and charity. He is by nature extraordinarily intelligent and doesn't allow ghosts. Tenacious in his opinions, he never yields and frustrates all who shield themselves in false goodness. They call him amoral and really he has nothing to do with those who admit laws or moral norms.

In the middle of the torment that clocks and calendars create for him, he tries to do and let be done what he considers fair in life: working and creating. He never scorns the value of others, but he defends himself, because he knows that this signifies rhythm and proportion with the world of reality. In exchange for giving pleasure, he gives pleasure; in exchange for effort, he gives effort. Being more qualified than others, he gives much more quantity and quality of sensitivity asking only understanding. Many times not even this is forthcoming. Many of the conflicts that his superior personality causes in daily life arise from this natural discontrol that provokes his revolutionary concepts. The problems that could be called domestic, that various women have been close to Diego, consists of the same thing. Diego has a profound consciousness of class and of the role of the other social classes in the functioning of the world. Of the persons who have lived near him, some want to be allied to the cause for which he works and fights, and others do not. From here originates a series of conflicts for which he is not responsible, since his position is clear and transparent. He is not responsible for the incapacity of the rest, nor for the consequences that this contributes to the social life. He works for order that all the forces organize themselves with a greater harmony.

With what arms can one struggle for or against a being who is nearer to reality? Naturally these weapons have to be amoral, rebels to what is already established or admitted as good or bad. I — with the fullness of my responsibility — figure that I cannot be against Diego, and if I am not one of his best allies, I wish I were. From my attitude in this portrait essay many things can be deduced, depending upon who deduces them; but my truth, the only one that I can give about Diego is this. Pure, unmeasurable in *sincere-meters** that don't exist, except in my conviction and my own experience.

No words will describe Diego's immense tenderness for things that have beauty; his affection for the beings who don't matter in the eyes of society; or his

Sincereometros is a word Frida made up. It means both *sincere-meters* and *without zero meters.*

105

de esperanza y caridad. Es por naturaleza extraordinariamente inteligente y no admite fantasmas. Tenaz en sus opiniones, nunca cede, y defrauda a todos los que se escudan en la creencia o en la falsa bondad. De aquí que le llamen amoral y – realmente – no tiene nada que ver con los que admiten las leyes o normas de la moral.

En medio del tormento que para él son el reloj y el calendario, trata de hacer y dejar hacer lo que él considera justo en la vida: trabajar y crear. Le da beligerancia a todas las otras direcciones, es decir, nunca menosprecia el valor de los demás, pero defiende el propio, porque sabe que éste significa ritmo y relación de proporciones con el mundo de la realidad. A cambio de placer, da placer; a cambio de esfuerzo, da esfuerzo. Estando más capacitado que los otros, da mucha mayor cantidad y calidad de sensibilidad pidiendo solamente entendimiento. Muchas veces ni esto consigue, pero no por esto se somete ni se rinde. Muchos de los conflictos que su personalidad superior causa en la vida diaria provienen de ese descontrol natural que provocan sus conceptos revolucionarios en relación a los ya sometidos a un rigor y a una norma. Los problemas que se pudieran llamar de hogar, que varias mujeres hemos tenido cerca de Diego, consisten en lo mismo. Diego tiene una profunda conciencia de clase y del papel que las otras clases sociales tienen en el funcionamiento general del mundo. De las personas que hemos vivido cerca de él, unas queremos ser aliadas de la causa por la que él trabaja y pelea, y otras no. De aquí se originan una serie de conflictos en los que él se ve mezclado, pero de los que no es responsable, puesto que su posición es clara y transparente. Su unidad humana, sin prejuicios, ya sea por genio, por educación o por transformación, no es responsable de la incapacidad de los demás, ni de las consecuencias que ésta aporte a la vida social. El trabaja para que todas las fuerzas se aprovechen y se organicen con una mayor armonía.

¿Con qué armas se puede luchar a favor o en contra de un ser que está más cerca de la realidad, más dentro de la verdad, si estas armas son morales, es decir, normadas según las conveniencias de determinada persona o sector humano? Naturalmente tienen que ser amorales, rebeldes a lo ya establecido o admitido como bueno o malo. Yo – con la plenitud de mi responsabilidad – estimo que no puedo estar en contra de Diego, y si no soy una de sus mejores aliadas, quisiera serlo. De mi actitud en este ensayo de retrato pueden deducirse muchas cosas, depende de quienes las deduzcan; pero mi verdad, la única que puedo dar acerca de Diego está aquí. Limpia, inmedible en sincerómetros, que no existen, sino con la convicción de lo que respecta a mí misma, mi propia experiencia.

Ningunas palabras describirán la inmensa ternura de Diego por las cosas que tienen belleza; su cariño por los seres que no tienen que ver en la presente sociedad

respect for those that are oppressed. He has special adoration for the Indians who are bound to him by blood; he loves them deeply, for their elegance, for their beauty and for being the living flower of the American cultural tradition. He loves children, all animals, with a predilection for Mexican hairless dogs and birds, plants and rocks. He loves all beings without being docile or neutral. He is very affectionate but never surrenders; for this, and because he hardly has time to dedicate himself to personal relations, they call him an ingrate. He is respectful and fine and nothing angers him more than abuse and the lack of respect of others. He cannot tolerate tricks or deceitful fraud or what in Mexico is called "pulling your leg." He would rather have intelligent enemies than stupid allies. He is rather merry by temperament, but it irritates him enormously when people waste his time while he is working. His amusement is his own work; he hates social reunions and he marvels at the truly popular fiestas. Sometimes he is shy, and as much as he is fascinated by conversation, he sometimes delights in being absolutely alone. He is never bored because everything interests him, studying, analyzing and being profound in all manifestations of life. He is not sentimental but is intensely emotional and passionate. Inertia exasperates him because he is a continual current, live and potent.

He admires and appreciates all that contains beauty, whether it thrives in a woman or a mountain. Perfectly balanced in all his emotions, sensations and deeds, which are moved by dialectic materialism, precise and real, he will never submit. Like the cactus on his land, he grows strong and astonishing, whether in sand or in rock. He flowers with the most alive red, the most transparent white and sun yellow. Cloaked in thorns, he keeps his tenderness inside. He lives with his strong sap inside a ferocious medium, giving light alone, like the avenging sun on gray rock. His roots live despite being uprooted, surviving the anguish of solitude, sadness and all the weaknesses that cause others to yield. He rises with surprising force and, like no other plant, he flourishes and gives fruit.

Frida Kahlo
translated by *Nancy Breslow and Amy Weiss Narea*

de clases; o su respeto por los que están oprimidos por la misma. Tiene especial adoración por los indios a quienes lo liga su sangre; los quiere entrañablemente, por su elegancia, por su belleza y por ser la flor viva de la tradición cultural de América. Quiere a los niños, a todos los animales, con predilección a los perros pelones mexicanos y a los pájaros, a las plantas y a las piedras. Ama a todos los seres sin ser dócil ni neutral. Es muy cariñoso pero nunca se entrega; por esto, y porque apenas tiene tiempo para dedicarse a las relaciones personales, le llaman ingrato. Es respetuoso y fino y nada le violenta más que la falta de respeto de los demás y el abuso. No soporta el truco o el engaño solapado; lo que en México se llama "tomadura de pelo." Prefiere tener enemigos inteligentes que aliados estúpidos. De temperamento es más bien alegre, pero le irrita enormemente que le quiten el tiempo en el trabajo. Su diversión es el trabajo mismo; odia las reuniones sociales y le maravillan las fiestas verdaderamente populares. A veces es tímido, y así como le fascina conversar y discutir con todos, le encanta a veces estar absolutamente solo. Nunca se aburre porque todo le interesa; estudiando, analizando y profundizando en todas las manifestaciones de la vida. No es sentimental pero sí intensamente emotivo y apasionado. Le desespera la inercia porque él es una corriente contínua, viva y potente. De buen gusto extraordinario, admira y aprecia todo lo que contiene belleza, lo mismo si vibra en una mujer o en una montaña. Perfectamente equilibrado en todas sus emociones, sus sensaciones y sus hechos, a los que mueve la dialéctica materialista, precisa y real, nunca se entrega. Como los cactus de su tierra, crece fuerte y asombroso, lo mismo en la arena que en la piedra; florece con el rojo más vivo, el blanco más transparente y el amarillo solar; revestido de espinas, resguarda dentro su ternura; vive con su savia fuerte dentro de un medio feroz; ilumina solitario como sol vengador del gris de la piedra; sus raíces viven a pesar de que lo arranquen de la tierra, sobrepasando la angustia de la soledad y de la tristeza y de todas las debilidades que a otros seres doblegan. Se levanta con sorprendente fuerza y, como ninguna otra planta, florece y da frutos.

Frida Kahlo

En su cárcel de espinos y rosas
cantan y juegan mis pobres niños.
hermosos seres desde la cuna
por la desgracia ya perseguidos.

En su cárcel se duermen soñando
cuán bello es el mundo cruel que no vieron,
cuán ancha la tierra, cuán hondos los mares,
cuán grande el espacio, qué breve su huerto.

Y le envidian las alas al pájaro
que transpone las cumbres y valles,
y le dicen: "¿Qué has visto allá lejos,
golondrina que cruzas los aires?"

Y despiertan soñando, y dormidos
        soñando se quedan:
que ya son la nube flotante que pasa,
o ya son el ave ligera que vuela,
tan lejos, tan lejos del nido, cual ellos
de su cárcel ir lejos quisieran.

"¡Todos parten! exclaman —. ¡Tan solo
tan solo nosotros nos quedamos siempre!
¿Por qué quedar, madre: por qué no llevarnos
donde hay otro cielo, otro aire, otras gentes?"

Yo, en tanto, bañados en llanto mis ojos,
los miro en silencio, pensando: "En la tierra,
¿adónde llevaros, mis pobres cautivos,
que no hayan de ataros las mismas cadenas?
Del hombre, enemigo del hombre, no puede
libraros, mis ángeles, la égida materna."

Rosalía de Castro

In their prison of buckthorn and roses
They sing and play, these poor children of mine,
Lovely creatures who, from the cradle,
Have been pursued by misfortune.

In their prison they sleep, dreaming
How beautiful is this cruel world they've never seen,
How wide the earth, how deep the seas,
How great the sky, how tiny this garden.

And they envy the bird its wings
That carry it over hills and distant valleys,
And they call to it, saying: "What have you seen,
Little swallow, friend of the winds?"

And they dream awake and sleep
Still dreaming;
Now they are a cloud drifting high,
Now they are a bird, flying lightly,
So far, so far from the nest, as they too
Far from this prison, would fly.

"Everybody goes!" they complain, "only we
Have to stay.
Why stay here, Mother? Why not take us
To another place with a different sky
And different faces?"

I, meanwhile, my eyes bathed with tears,
Look at them in silence, thinking: "On this earth,
Where could I take you, my poor little captives,
Where the same chains would not bind you?
From man, enemy of man, my angels,
Not even a mother's love can free you."

Rosalía de Castro
translated by *Barbara Dale May*

蝶戀花　憶女　楊濤

欹枕呻吟清不寐　病入人心　藥石
爐空沸　慘淡寒燈天欲曙　依稀殘
夢輕輕記　一片雞聲和　夜雨攬亂
愁腸　總是傷心味　千徧思量千徧
淚　何時得汝欣欣至。

Calligraphy by Yang Toa-Ping

112

THINKING OF MY DAUGHTER
Tz'u to the tune of Tieh Lien Hua "Butterflies Love Flowers"

I groan as I lean
    wide-awake on my pillow.
When disease enters the heart
It is useless to boil herbs and stones.
The lamp is cold and desolate,
    the sky about to break.
Only a little is left of a dream
    that is too faint to recall.

The cocks crow together
    through the sound of the night rain.
My aching flesh is shaken by that,
Feels throughout like a broken heart.
I think it over a thousand times,
    a thousand times I cry:
When will I see you
    coming home in joy?

Yang Ch'e
translated by *Li Chi and Michael O'Connor*

רָחֵל בָּכְתָה שָׁם אֶת בָּנֶיהָ

רָחֵל בָּכְתָה שָׁם אֶת בָּנֶיהָ שֶׁטֶרֶם נוֹלְדוּ
וְטֶרֶם תִּינוֹקוֹת הָיוּ רְפֵי פָּנִים שֶׁאִמָּהוֹת אֲלֵיהֶם נְמוֹגוֹת.
בַּשָּׂדֶה עָמְדָה אֶל הָרוּחַ, שְׁקוּפָה פְּצֵלָה,
וּבְשָׂרָהּ הָיָה עִם הָאֲדָמָה
יוֹסֵף וּבִנְיָמִין כְּבָר הָיוּ רְגָבִים
וְהִיא בָּכְתָה אֶת בָּנֶיהָ מוּל הַגְּבָעוֹת.
רָחֵל בָּכְתָה אֶת בָּנֶיהָ
בְּטֶרֶם לִבְכּוֹת יָדְעוּ
בְּטֶרֶם מִן הֶעָפָר גָּחוּ
כְּדֵי אֵלָיו לָשׁוּב.

אוֹ אוּלַי בָּכְתָה רָחֵל אֶת בָּנֶיהָ אַחֲרֵי מוֹתָם
כְּשֶׁנַּחוּ כְּאַבְקָנִים חוּרִים בְּרָאשֵׁי הַגִּבְעוֹל
וְקִבְרָהּ הָרָחָב פָּתוּחַ מֵאַרְבַּע רוּחוֹת לְכַנְּסָם
וּזְרוֹעוֹתֶיהָ הָרְחָבוֹת פְּתוּחוֹת אוֹתָם לִקְלֹט
וְהֵם מְרַחֲפִים בִּדְמָמָה אֶל תּוֹךְ בְּכִיהָ
כְּאֶל תּוֹךְ גְּבוּלָם.

רִבְקָה מִרְיָם

RACHEL CRIED THERE FOR HER CHILDREN

Rachel cried there for her children not yet born
not yet soft-faced infants whose mothers melt to them.
In the field she stood to the wind,
transparent as her shadow,
and her flesh was with the soil.
Joseph and Benjamin already clods
and she cried for her children against the hills.
Rachel cried for her children
before they knew how to cry
before they burst from the dust
to return to it.

       * * * * *

or perhaps Rachel cried for her sons after their deaths
as they rested like pale stamens at the head of the stem
her wide grave opened to the winds collecting them
her arms opened wide to absorb them
and they hovered quietly into her cry
as into their border.

Rivka Miriam
translated by *Linda Zisquit*

INTRODUCTION

What follows is an excerpt from a tale told by Charles Cultee in 1890 to ethnologist Franz Boas. At the time of the recording, Cultee was one of three remaining speakers of the Kathlamet language, a dialect of the Upper Chinook peoples living on the Columbia River "from Astoria on the south side and Grey's Harbor on the north side of the river to Rainier." (Boas.) Scant anthropological information exists on the Kathlamet-speaking tribes. Nonetheless, because of Boas' work in the Pacific Northwest, many myths and tales have been preserved. Most of these texts have remained buried in the old Bulletins of the Bureau of American Ethnology, dated from around the turn of the century. Moreover, the English renderings offered there by Boas are all in prose.

Yet what we are dealing with here is an *oral* tradition from a tightly organized language community. Native listeners to this tale would have heard this and other versions many times in the course of a lifetime, the layers and variations blending in a rich understanding and appreciation of the theme and the individual style of the performer. And performers they were — for recitation of myths and tales of this and much longer lengths was an art, closely akin to a dramatic or poetic reading. One goal of this translation has been, therefore, to restore to an English version of the tale as much of its original poetic style as possible.

At the same time, an accurate translation of content and meaning has also been a central concern. Without fuller ethnographic material on the Kathlamet speakers, of course, we cannot be completely certain of symbolism in the tale. But, by comparing it to similar stories in sister languages and by placing this excerpt in the context of the complete tale (Part Two is not included herein), several patterns emerge. Imagistically, for example, berry picking and shells are obviously identified with females and their role in society. Similarly, hunting and arrows are identified with males and their role. Numbers which hold deep ritual significance are both five and three. The reader will notice, for instance, that the maiden leaves her home five times before discovering her children's trickery.

In terms of theme, it is most often the case that the "subject" of Northwest Native tales is not the main character. That is to say, this is not a story about a woman who goes wrong (or right, for that matter). Instead, the reader can consider the tribe or tribal grouping represented by family as the subject of the tale. With that in mind, the theme is one of deviance and how that is handled in the context of a given social, physical and spiritual environment.This is a story about change and the regeneration of tradition, about being an individual in a communal society.

Joan Boisclair
September, 1980

116

TIAPEXOACXOAC — A girl has a bitch. While she is away, it is killed and the fat is given to her to eat. She is deserted by the tribe. Then she gives birth to five male dogs and one female. When she is away, the dogs assume the shape of children. Finally she discovers their transformation and burns their dogskin blankets. The boys become great hunters. Tiapexoacxoac hears about her daughter. He is a great chief who eats his wives. He kills all his male children. The brothers kill a sea monster, and give the blood to him to drink. He cannot drink it all, and for that reason makes peace with the brothers. He marries the girl, who gives birth to a boy. She escapes with the baby. The boy grows up in the woods and becomes stronger than his father, whom he resembles in every respect. One day he goes to his father's house, and is mistaken for Tiapexoacxoac himself. The latter sends slaves to search for him. The son kills all the people. Then Tiapexoacxoac requests him to come back. The boy agrees, and when he returns, his sons shoot their grandfather. (Abstract of Tale by *Franz Boas*)

A'qa ēXā't afiā'tjau. A'qa itcō'mEla ictā'muX; a'qa itcō'cgam.
Then   one   maiden.   Then   he bought   a chief;   then   he took her.
                                 her   1

Nīct tqjäx igī'vux. A'qa guā'nEsum agā'kjōtkōt qacqLqō'yōXuîtx.
Not like she did him. Then always   her bitch   they two slept together. 2

Qā'mta nō'îx guā'nEsum agō'kīx agā'kjōtkōt. Guā'nEsum itjō'kti
Where she went always she carried her her bitch.   Always   good   3

iLxE'lEm agialqō'emuX agā'kjōtkōt. A'qa agā'pXEleu agā'kjōtkōt.
food she gave it to eat to her her bitch.   Then   her fat   her bitch.   4

Ā'qa igā'elalakuit. A'qa igē'kîm itcā'kikal: "Ai'aq amcgō'waq
Then   she forgot her. Then he said her husband: "Quick   kill her   5

agā'kjōtkōt." A'qa iLgō'waq Liā'wuXikc itcā'kikal. A'qa
her bitch."   Then they killed her his brothers her husband.   Then   6

iLgaxLE'lam. Lä+ aqa iLE'kōtcXEm. Môkct tkci agā'pXEleu.
they singed her. Long then they boiled her. **Two** fingers her fat.   7

A'qa iqagE'lōtk agā'kjōtkōt. A'qa igaXatkjoā'mam. Tsō'yustîX
Then it was put aside her bitch.   Then **she came home.**   In the evening   8

igaXatkjoā'mam. A'qa igō'lXam agā'tōm: "Aqē'sgoax itcō'waq;
she came home. Then she said to her her sister-in-law: "A seal he killed it;   9

imē'pōtcxan itcō'waq. Tau'wax iqamgE'lōtk." Lqjōp igī'vuX
your brother-in-law he killed it. This was put aside for you." Cut   she did it   10

itcā'pXEleu. Igē'wîlqj. Igō'n wi ēXt igē'wîlqj. Qoä'nEma Lq!ōp
its fat.   She ate it. Another also one she ate it. Five   cuts   11

igē'wîlqj. A'qa ē'mqōlkī itcō'xoa. A'qa iā'c igī'vux. "Ō,
she ate them. Then qualmishness did her. Then let she did it. "Oh,   12
                                            alone

LXuan ta'u agE'kjōtkōt iqanE'lqoēm."
maybe this my bitch was given to me to eat."   13

Note: This is a reproduction of page 155 of Bulletin 26 of the Bureau of American Ethnology in which Franz Boas' phonetic transcriptions and translations of Kathlamet Texts are published. We include the abstract for the reader's information.

TIAPEXOASXOAS

Part One

i. Now there was a maiden.
        Now a chief bought her.
        Now he took her.
    She did not like him.
        Now always she and her bitch, they two slept together.
        Whenever she went, always she carried her bitch.
        Always good food she gave it to eat.
        Now fat was her bitch.
    Now one day she forgot her bitch.
    Now her husband said:
        "Quick! Kill her bitch!"
    Now his brothers, they killed her.
        Now they singed her.
        Long now they boiled her.
        Two fingers thick was her fat.
        Now it was put aside, her bitch.

    Now the woman came home.
        In the evening, she came home.
    Now her sister-in-law said to her:
        "A seal, he killed it;
        your brother-in-law, he killed it.
        This was put aside for you."
    She cut its fat.
        She ate it.
        Another piece also she ate.
        Five pieces she ate.
    Now she felt squeamish.
        Now she let it alone.
        "Oh, maybe this was my bitch given to me to eat."
    Long after now pregnancy was on her.

    Now he was ashamed, her husband.
        "Perhaps another made her pregnant.
        It was not I.
        It is good that we leave her."
    Now again she went to pick berries.

Now they left her.
　　　They carried away all their houses.
　　　They broke all their old canoes.
In the evening, she came home.
　　　Now there were no people.
　　　"Oh now look!
　　　I am deserted."
Now she made a small house.
　　　Now there she stayed.

ii.　Long after now she gave birth.
　　　She gave birth to a dog.
　　　Now she kicked it.
Now she gave birth to another one, again a dog.
　　　Five male dogs, one female, she gave birth to them.
Now she suckled them.
　　　Now large they became.

Now always she left them at the house.
Now one day she found boys' tracks toward the water from her house.
　　　"Where may these boys have come from?"
She came in;
　　　there were her children.

Another day she went.
　　　In the evening, she came home.
Now there were many boys' tracks.
　　　Now there lay an arrow.
　　　She took it.
Now there lay a shell.
　　　She took it.
　　　She thought:
　　　"Look! A girl child."
She thought:
　　　"Maybe they will be killed, my dogs."
She came in;
　　　there were her dogs.

Now day came again.

Now again she went;
    she picked berries.
In the evening, now again, she came home.
    Oh now there were many boys' tracks.
    There were many arrows.
    Now there lay shells.
    Many lay there.
    "Where may these boys have come from?"
She came in;
    there were her dogs.
Next day, she went again;
    she went picking berries.
    Near she went.
    Now there she picked berries.
Now she heard the boys.
While the sun was still up, now, she went home.
    "Oh, quick! I will go home.
    Perhaps they will be killed, my dogs."
    Now she went home.
Now she came home; no boys.
    Now soft was the beach with their tracks.
She came in;
    there were her dogs.
    She thought:
    "Tomorrow, now, I will hide."

iii. Day came;
    she made herself ready.
    She went out;
    she stayed in the grass.
Soon, now, she heard the boys in the house.
    Soon, now, a girl came out.
    She went around the house.
    Now again she entered.
"Well, did you see our mother?"
"Long ago she went;
    nobody is outside."
Soon, now, a boy went out.

Another one went out.
Another again went out.
Five boys went out and one girl.
At once they went seaward.

She entered the house, that woman.
Now she saw them, their blankets, their dog blankets.
She took them;
she burned them.
Now she went seaward.
"Oh, my children, why have you disguised yourselves before
me?
Quick, let us go up from the beach."
Now they hid their faces, all.
Twice she spoke to them, her children.
Now the five went up.
One had a bad leg;
long he did not go up.
In the evening, now he also went up.

Now they stayed, her children.
Now large they became, her children.
Now always she and her daughter, they two picked berries.
Long after now all (her sons) became hunters;
one, deer his game;
one, elk his game;
one, seals his game;
one, sturgeon his game;
one, sea lions his game.

Kathlamet Tale (recorded 1890)
translated by *Joan Boisclair*

PAULINCHEN WAR ALLEIN ZU HAUS

Das war seine übliche Unterbrechung in der Nacht. Das Kind versuchte, schläfrig zu bleiben, auch diesmal. Allerdings war der Befehl *Schläfrigbleiben* schon eine kleine Tat im Kopf. Der Kopf mußte den Befehl denken. Der Befehl machte eigentlich schon etwas zu wach. Das Kind mußte schließlich außerdem darauf achten, daß nur der Befehl *Schläfrigbleiben* im Kopf und darin allein war. Das war seine übliche schwierige Unterbrechung in der Nacht.

Einen Nachttopf neben dem Bett und damit einen kürzeren Vorgang, einen ohne langwierige Befehle und Befolgungen, war vom Kind mit Entschiedenheit abgelehnt worden. Als das Kind noch bei den Großeltern wohnte, hatte es überhaupt nie einen Gedanken an die nächtlichen Unterbrechungen verloren. Fast waren das gar keine Unterbrechungen. Es konnte meistens im Zusammenhang mit einem Traum bleiben, wenn es sich nach der Erleichterung auf dem Nachttopf wieder zurückwühlte in seine Nacht im Bett. Falls es aber doch mal etwas wacher wurde und nicht gleich weiterschlafen konnte, genoß es diesen Zustand mit der zurückkommenden Wärme und Schläfrigkeit. Es hatte ihn besonders gern. Es versuchte, sich in einem so wohligen Halbschlaf halbwach zu halten.

Seit seiner Übernahme durch Christa und Kurt ließ es nicht mehr mit sich reden, zum Kapitel *Nachttopf*. Hör mal, sagten die Erwachsenen freundlich, wir beide haben den gesamten Problemkomplex neu durchdacht, kann sein, daß wir uns geirrt haben, auch Erwachsene irren sich. Das Kind hörte diese spezielle neugierige Geduld aus den Stimmen der Erwachsenen. Es spürte die Beobachtung der zwei Erwachsenen richtig auf der Haut.

Das ist ja nun vorläufig mal egal, ob du nun schon zu groß bist für so was oder nicht. Du bist vorläufig mal dran gewöhnt, nachts aufs Töpfchen zu gehen, und wir wollen nicht drüber herziehen, ob da deine Großeltern einen Fehler gemacht haben oder nicht.

Ich brauche keinen Nachttopf, sagte das Kind. Ich hätte sowieso keinen gebraucht. Ich hätte sowieso damit aufgehört. Es sagte mit Absicht *Nachttopf* und nicht *Töpfchen* wie Christa, denn Christa hatte sich ja nur verstellt und meinte mit einem erwachsenen Ekel *Topf, Nachttopf*.

Das stimmt ja alles nicht, sagte Christa. Warum verdrängst du schon wieder was, sagte Kurt. Was denn? Du verdrängst immer mal wieder, immer wenn dir was peinlich ist, die Wahrheit. Die Wahrheit ist aber das Wichtigste. Für dich und auch für uns, denn wir sind es, die dich kennenlernen müssen, und wollen, kennenlernen, ja, und zwar ganz so, wie du bist.

"Die E.," schrieb das Kind ins blaue Heft und machte einen Doppelpunkt hinter das "E." E stand für *Eltern*. Es wollte nicht *Eltern* schreiben. Das blaue Heft war das

LITTLE PAULINE WAS ALONE AT HOME
(An excerpt from the novel)

This was her customary interruption in the night. The child tried, this time too, to remain sleepy. Certainly the command *stay sleepy* had already been acted out in her brain. The brain had to think the command. Really the command was responsible for making her somewhat too wakeful. Ultimately, it was up to the child to make sure that the command *stay sleepy,* remain separated in her head. This was her customary interruption in the night.

A chamberpot next to the bed providing a shorter procedure, one without tedious commands and compliances, was emphatically rejected by the child. While the child still lived with the grandparents, she absolutely never gave a thought to the nightly interruptions. They almost weren't interruptions. She could usually remain linked with a dream, provided after the relief on the chamberpot the child burrowed back into her night in bed. If she, however, occasionally did become wakeful and could not go back to sleep immediately, she enjoyed the condition of returning warmth and sleepiness. She liked that particularly well. She tried to maintain a pleasant state of half sleep, half wakefulness.

Since her take-over by Christa and Kurt, she would no longer speak on the *Chamberpot* subject. Listen, the grownups said in a friendly manner, we have both thought through the whole complex problem anew, could be that we erred, even grownups err. The child heard that special curious patience in the voices of the adults. The feeling of being observed by the two adults really gave her gooseflesh.

Meanwhile it is irrelevant whether or not you are already too big for such a thing. Right now you are used to using the potty at night and we do not want to know that or argue about whether or not your grandparents made an error.

I don't need a chamberpot, the child said. I would not have needed it anyway. I would have stopped with it anyway. She said *chamberpot* on purpose and not *potty,* like Christa, because Christa was only dissimulating and meant, with adult disgust *pot, chamberpot.*

None of that is correct, Christa said. Why are you repressing something again, Kurt said. What? You are repressing the truth, as always when something is painful for you. Yet the truth is paramount. For you and for us, since we are the ones who must get to know you, and want to get to know you, completely, the real you.

"The P.," the child wrote in the blue exercise book, and put a colon behind the "P." P stood for *Parents.* She did not want to write *Parents.* The blue exercise book

Heft für die Einfälle und für die eiligen Notizen. Was davon zu verwerten war, kam später in ein gelbes Heft. "Die E.: behaupten ja nur, daß sie mich kennenlernen wollen. Sie wollen mich überhaupt nicht kennenlernen." Das Kind war mit seiner Niederschrift nicht zufrieden. Irgendwas stimmte nicht, nicht ganz, noch nicht, noch nicht einmal als Bruchstück und Eilnotiz. Etwas fehlte. Es war ihm selber oft nicht klar: wollte es sich denn kennenlernen lassen ganz so wie es war? Manchmal schon. Dann wieder ganz und gar nicht. Manchmal aber. Dann ließ es den Anfang von einer Wahrheit über sich heraus. Entweder ergab sich aus dem Anfang gleich und sofort eine Enttäuschung und das Kind fühlte sich zurückgestoßen. Oder der Wahrheitsanfang wurde gleich und sofort begierig von diesen "E." aufgegriffen und sie fingen wieder an zu reden, und so ein Reden dauerte, dauerte. Nie hatte das Kind erlebt, daß was Schönes und Wichtiges und Erlösendes für es selber bei diesem endlosen Hin und Her von Sätzen herauskam.

Also, wie stehts nun, bist du noch immer eingeschnappt? Wegen des blöden unwichtigen Nachttopfgeschichtchens? *Sie ist entsetzlich leicht beleidigt. Sie schnappt allzu rasch ein.* Wir fanden das nur einen Augenblick lang ein bißchen merkwürdig, den *Topf,* meine Liebe, wir, Kurt und ich, das mußt du doch verstehen, denn normalerweise gehen Mädchen in deinem Alter nicht mehr auf einen Nachttopf. Buben übrigens erst recht nicht, und du willst ja immer ein *Paul* sein. Also bitte. Aber wir haben gelernt, umgelernt, wir sehen das jetzt neu und unbefangen. Das Kind verweigerte nunmehr mit seinem wirksamen Material *Stummheit, Wegblicken, Wegtrotten, Was-Anderes-Machen* jegliche Stellungnahme zum Nachttopfthema. *Da: Sie sieht ja geradezu verkniffen aus.*

*　*　*　*　*

Ach, meine Großeltern, dachte das Kind, es nahm sich vor, etwas über die Großeltern zu notieren. Es mußte mit *Ach* anfangen. Etwas über die gemütlichen geborgenen Nächte, auch über die Tage in den kleineren gemütlichen Zimmern dort mit den altmodischen Möbeln und Bildern, aber vor allem über ein Gefühl wollte es schreiben, und zuvor darüber nachdenken, oder danach nachdenken, über ein Gefühl, das es bei Christa und Kurt oft geradezu einschnürte, richtig zusammen-preßte. Vorher nie erlebt. Scham. Beschämung. Scham, wie Schimpf und Schande. Bei den Großeltern hat das Kind einfach den Nachttopf benutzt, sonst nichts. Bei Christa und Kurt empfand das Kind, daß es überhaupt nichts mehr selbstverständlich tat. Es mußte jetzt jeweils, bevor es etwas tat, überlegen, über-denken, überprüfen. Das Kind hat sich bei den Großeltern nicht so viel Zeit stehlen lassen, sondern Zeit gehabt für eine andere Nachdenklichkeit. Die war ihm wichtig und die war unvorsichtig und unabhängig von Alltagssachen. Es dachte, etwas in der Art müsse es ins blaue Heft schreiben. Es wollte aber nicht, daß das Wort *Nachttopf* im blauen Heft vorkäme. Das Wort wollte es gar nicht erst hinschreiben.

was the exercise book for ideas and for quick notes. What was useable was later transferred to a yellow exercise book. "The P. only allege that they want to get to know me. They do not want to get to know me at all." The child was not satisfied with her notes. Something did not sound right, not entirely, not yet, not even as a fragmentary and quick note. Something was missing. It was often not even clear to her: did she want them to get to know the way she really was? Sometimes yes. Then again not at all. Sometimes however. Then she allowed the beginning of a truth to come out.

Either right at the start there was a disappointment and the child felt rejected. Or the beginning of a truth was immediately eagerly seized by the "P." and they started to talk again, and such talk went on and on. It had never been the child's experience that something beautiful and important and uplifting emerged for herself from the endless interchange of sentences.

Well, how do things stand now, are you still sulking? Because of the stupid, unimportant chamberpot business? *She is dreadfully easily offended. She sulks all too easily.* We only found it mildly noteworthy for a moment, the *pot,* my love, we, Kurt and I, you should certainly understand that, because normally girls of your age do not use a chamberpot any more. Boys even less, and you always want to be a *Paul.* So please. But we have learned, relearned, we now see it in a new light, without embarrassment. The child refused each further overture on the chamberpot theme, using her effective equipment *silence, looking away, walking away, do-something else. There: right away she looks uptight.*

* * * * *

Oh, my grandparents, thought the child, planning to make some notes on the grandparents. It must begin with *Oh.* Something about the cozy, secure nights, also about the days in the little cozy rooms there with the old-fashioned furniture and pictures, but above all she wanted to write about a feeling, and first to think about it, or to think about it afterwards, about a feeling, with Christa and Kurt that often choked, really squeezed. Never before experienced. Shame. Being shamed. Shame, like insult and disgrace. At her grandparents the child simply used the chamberpot, that was all. With Christa and Kurt, the child sensed that she could do nothing naturally anymore. Now, suddenly, before she did anything, she had to consider, think it over, check it out. The child had not allowed herself to waste that much time at her grandparents, rather she had time for other meditation. It was imprudent and unrelated to everyday matters, but it was important matters. She thought, she should write something like that in the blue exercise book. She did not want the word *chamberpot* to appear in the blue

Damit jedoch ließ es etwas von der Wahrheit weg. Was war denn los mit ihm und der Wahrheit? Es erschrak. Es war doch immer so beruhigt darüber, daß wenigstens die Schreibhefte Geheimplätze für die Wahrheit waren. Der Nachttopf mußte schon vorkommen, vielleicht konnte man das alles anders ausdrücken, vielleicht irgendwie medizinisch. Es bekam auch Lust, die Großeltern in die Eltern umzumodeln, und zwar in die wahren, richtigen Eltern, mit denen es verwandt war. "Ach meine Eltern, ihr seid tot/Ach euer Kind: ich bin in Not." Das war schon ziemlich rührend und ganz gut. So ganz einfach. Das Kind wartete vergeblich sehnsüchtig auf ein paar Tränen. Zu seinem Leidwesen konnte es nicht oft genug weinen, gerade dann nicht, wenn es dringend weinen wollte. "Als ich dann in die Welt raus kam/Empfand ich Angst und Pein und Scham." Die beiden Zeilen gefielen dem Kind nicht so gut. "…raus kam" war zu gewöhnlich. Alles was stimmte, war das Versmaß. Beim Weiterdenken empfand es, daß der entscheidende Fehler seines Klagelieds der war: "…ihr seid tot." So trostlos stellte das Kind sich den Zustand der wahren Eltern nicht vor. Es glaubte, manchmal mit Absicht unter dem Begriff *fromm, ich bin enorm fromm,* manchmal aber auch einfach so, einfach selbstverständlich, daß es den Eltern gut ging, anderswo. Die überlebten, fast garantiert. *Wir haben die gesamten Kirchen Wiens abgeklappert, die kleine Paula immer brav und still hinterher,* erzählten Christa und Kurt den Bekannten nach einer Wien-Reise. Sie hat sich niemals beklagt? *Nein nie, von einer Kirche zur andern.* Sie ist schon ein Schatz, wir könnens gut mal wieder wagen, z. B. mit Rom, wo es ja noch ein ganzes Stück anstrengender wird mit Kirchen und so für eine Achtjährige. Sogar für erwachsene Leute. Das Kind schrieb ins blaue Heft: "Ich habe die ganzen Kirchen von Wien abgeklappert und nach dem richtigen Altar mit der richtigen Stimmung gesucht und so weiter." "Und so weiter" würde im gelben Heft ausgefüllt. "Ich habe von einer Kirche zur andern immer nur nach dem Tisch des Herrn gesucht, nach dem richtigen Tisch in der richtigen Beleuchtung mit dem richtigen Drumherum." "Drumherum" würde auch im gelben Heft ein schöneres Wort, vielleicht bedürfte es mehrerer Wörter statt des *Drumherum.* "Dort im Michaeler fand ich den Tisch des Herrn. Meine Eltern und meine Geschwister waren nur gerade nicht da. Der Tisch des Herrn war für meine Geschwister zum Tee gedeckt. Ein schöner Teetisch. Sogar für die Großeltern war schon vorsichtshalber Platz gemacht. Sogar mein Gedeck war schon vorgesehen. Mein Platz, auch wenn es dann etwas eng werde wird. Meine Eltern Fühlen sich sehr wohl am Tisch des Herrn. Sie haben es jetzt dauernd schön und ruhig. Sie haben keine Sorgen. Das ist gar nicht in Wien, das war nur, damit ich es mal weiß, für mich kurz in Wien so gemacht, in Wirklichkeit ist es im Himmel, aber es sieht so aus wie in der Michaelerkirche."

*   *   *   *   *

exercise book however. In the first place she did not want to write the word down at all. Still that meant leaving out some of the truth. What was happening with her and the truth? She started. She had always been reassured that at least the writing pads were hiding places for the truth. The chamberpot should appear, perhaps one could express it all another way, perhaps somehow in medical terms. She was also tempted to remodel the parents into the grandparents, and indeed the true, real parents, to whom she was related. "Oh my parents, you are dead/oh your child: I am in need." That was already fairly stirring and quite good. Quite simple. The child waited in vain longing for a few tears. To her regret she could not cry often enough, especially not then, when she urgently wanted to cry. "When out into the world I came/I found fear and pain and shame." Those two lines did not appeal to the child too much. ". . .out came" was too ordinary. All that worked was the rhyme. With further thought she found that the decisive mistake of her lament was: ". . .you are dead." The child did not visualize the condition of her parents as that hopeless. She believed, sometimes purposely under the delusion *pious, I am terribly pious,* but sometimes only simply so, simply as a matter of course, that her parents were well, somewhere else. They survived, it is almost guaranteed. *We have knocked off all of the churches in Vienna, little Paula always good and quiet behind us,* Christa and Kurt told friends after a trip to Vienna. She never complained? *No never, from one church to another.* She is really a darling, we can well risk it again, for example with Rome, where it becomes still a good bit more strenuous with churches and so on for an eight year old. Even for grown people. The child wrote in the blue exercise book: "I knocked off all the churches in Vienna and searched for the right altar with the right mood and so forth." "And so forth" would be filled in in the yellow exercise book. "From one church to another I always only searched for the table of the Lord, for the right table in the right light with the right accessories." "Accessories" would also become a prettier word in the yellow exercise book, perhaps it would require several words instead of *accessories.* "There in the Michaeler I found the Lord's table. My parents and my siblings just happened not to be there. The Lord's table was set for my siblings for tea. A pretty tea table. There were even places set for my grandparents just in case. Even my place setting was anticipated. My place, even if it does make things a bit tight. My parents feel very comfortable at the Lord's table. They now always have peace and quiet. They have no worries. It is not even in Vienna, it was only just done for me in Vienna, so that I know about it, in reality it is in Heaven, but it looks like the one in the Michaeler church."

* * * * *

Weder in der Nacht beim Gebrauch des Nachttopfs, noch morgens, wenn das ein Anblick war, hat das Kind sich Gedanken über so Alltäglichkeiten wie Nachttopfbenutzen gemacht. Was für blöde Aufenthalte in seinem Kopf, mit dem es ständig viel Wichtigeres vorhatte. Sogar das Ausleeren und wer das machte, die Großmutter oder es selber: dem Kind egal. Wie absonderlich das in den Augen vernünftiger Menschen war, mußte das Kind erst erfahren. Christa und Kurt waren vernünftige Menschen, denn Christa sagte sehr oft *wir sind vernünftige Menschen,* und das Kind glaubte ihr aufs Wort. Es hatte nur sofort eine stinkwut auf *vernünftige Menschen.* Du wirst auch eines Tages ein vernünftiger Mensch werden, verhieß Christa ihm. Das Kind beschloß, mit jeder Willenskraft, die es besaß, kein *vernünftiger Mensch* zu werden. Erst recht dann, wenn Christa es in einen von diesen *Lernprozessen* hineinzog, es sich wieder mal in aller Ruhe und Besonnenheit verknöpfte. Seit dem Zusammenleben mit Christa und Kurt machte es ständig irgendwelche Erfahrungen mit sich, die es lehrten, daß es eigentlich ziemlich oft *absonderlich* war. Nur immer diese Ausrutscher, verdammt, mitten im Widerstand. Zu oft passiert es mir, dachte das Kind, daß ich den beiden dann doch gefallen will und zwar ganz enorm gefallen. Scheußlich. Ich bereue es jedesmal. Denn wenn ich ihnen gefalle, machen sie gleich weiter und reden und wollen so einen Fortschritt. Dann muß ich gleich noch was von mir aufgeben, von früher, und mich von etwas, das ich bin, trennen, von noch mehr. Miserabel. Ich will mal tagelang durchhalten und ihnen nicht und nie gefallen. Ich will ihnen mal tagelang furchtbar mißfallen.

*　*　*　*　*

Aber weißt du, Paula-Schatz, gerade Leute, die wirklich vernünftig sind so wie wir, die können, ja, die *müssen* gelegentlich auch mal ganz unvernünftig sein. Also: über die Stränge schlagen, wie man das nennt, mal was tun, das gegen die Prinzipien verstößt, aber nicht gegen die wirklich wichtigen Prinzipien – ich meine: die Grundsätze, die ein jeder haben muß, damit sie sein Leben untermauern und festigen. Nur wenn einer innerlich mit solchen Grundsätzen in diesem Sinn, den wir meinen, vernünftig ist, dann darf und soll er auch hin und wieder einen *un*vernünftigen Schlenker machen. Versteht du uns?

Das Kind sagte zuerst *nein.* Als die Erklärungsprofis fast froh daraufhin fortfuhren mit ganz ähnlichen und immer weiter ausholenden Sätzen und als das Kind eine Art Ohrenschmerzen bekam von den behutsam überdeutlichen Stimmen, als eine unerklärliche Geräuschempfindlichkeit ihm zu schaffen machte, bis ihm sozusagen der ganze Körper wehtat, sagte es *ja* und es habe alles verstanden und danach, als die Schmerzen vergingen, spürte es wieder die ihm etwas unheimliche Lust, diese Erwachsenen zu verärgern, *verärgern* ging, *quälen* ging beinah nie. Das Kind sagte: Ihr meint, Ehebruch und so etwas. Das ist unvernünftig und ihr müßt es manchmal machen. Christa und Kurt verhandelten später noch öfter über diese

Neither in the night while using the chamberpot, nor mornings, when it was a sight, did the child ponder such mundanities as the use of chamberpots. What imbecilic distractions in a head, constantly planning more important things. Even emptying it and who did it, the grandmother or herself: it was all the same to the child. How peculiar this was in the eyes of sensible people, the child had yet to learn. Christa and Kurt were sensible people, because Christa often said *we are sensible people,* and the child took her word for it. Only she immediately developed an unholy fury against *sensible people.* You will also become a sensible person one day, Christa assured her. The child resolved, with all the willpower she possessed, never to become a *sensible person.*

Especially when Christa incorporated it into one of those *learning experiences,* bringing it up once more in peace and quiet. Since the living together with Christa and Kurt she continuously had experiences which taught her that actually, she was actually often quite *strange.* Only these constant derailments, dammit, in the middle of resistance. It happens to me too often, thought the child, that I do want to please the two of them and please them enormously at that. Atrocious. I regret it each time. Because when I please them, they immediately go further and talk and want more progress. Then I must immediately sacrifice something of myself, from before, and disconnect myself from something that I am, from still more. Miserable. Sometimes I want to hold out for days and not please them, ever. Sometimes I want to displease them dreadfully for days.

* * * * *

But do you know, Paul-darling, that it is particularly people who are really sensible like us who can, yes, they *must* occasionally be completely irrational. So: kick over the traces, as one says, sometimes do something against one's principles, but not the truly important principles—I mean: the groundrules that everyone must have to maintain and fortify the foundations of their lives. Only when one has internalized those sensible basics in the way that we mean, then can and should one now and again make an *ir*rational move. Do you understand us?

At first the child said *no.* When the professional explanors continued almost happily with very similar and still more far-fetched sentences and when the child got a kind of earache from the careful, overemphatic voices, when an inexplicable noise sensitivity gave the child trouble until practically her whole body ached, she said *yes* and she understood everything and after that, when the pain left, she again felt the somewhat weird urge to anger these adults, *anger* worked, *torturing* almost never did. The child said: you mean, adultery and suchlike. That is irrational

Äußerung vom Kind. Leider haben wir wahrscheinlich unsere Reaktion nicht gut genug unter Kontrolle gehabt. *Du* zumindest hast ziemlich entgeistert ausgesehen. *Du* wenigstens hast reichlich empört gewirkt. *Du* hast da einen entscheidenden Fehler gemacht. *Du* bist leider überhaupt nicht gelassen geblieben. Aber wir haben uns doch bemerkenswert rasch wieder im Griff gehabt. Ist sie ein bißchen gemein, manchmal, die kleine Paula? Was hat sie denn bezweckt? Kurt, ich wage zu behaupten, sie hat diese Studentin aus Erlangen gemeint. Meine liebe Christa, du solltest dein Geknutsche mit Ernesto ein bißchen – na ja, sie beobachtet scharf, und sowieso ist es absolut unnötig, wie ihr zwei euch immer in den Armen liegt und euch abküßt. Auch scheint sie unsere Post zu lesen. Sofern du manchmal unsere Post liest, Paula, laß dich durch irgendwelche Verehrerbriefe nicht irreleiten. Es gibt Menschen, denen das, was wir schreiben, sehr am Herzen liegt und so weiter. Sie fühlen sich uns verwandt und so. Es ist außerdem eigentlich nicht schön, in der Post zu lesen, die an andere Personen gerichtet ist. Weil wir dir *grundsätzlich* nichts verbieten, meine Liebe, gehst du bedauerlicherweise gelegentlich etwas zu weit. Was nicht ausdrücklich *verboten* ist, ist nicht gleich ausdrücklich *erlaubt,* ja? Was soll man tun. Wir müssen deine kleinen Untaten, deine kleinen Geschmacklosigkeiten wohl oder übel in Kauf nehmen. Doch wäre es schöner für uns alle drei, wenn auch du dich partnerschaftlich verhalten würdest. Das Wort versteht sie doch wieder nicht, sagte Kurt zu Christa. Christa sagte: Wie ein Kamerad, wie unser Kamerad, so sollst du zu uns stehen, wie wir, Kurt und ich, seit vielen Jahren zueinander stehen. Wir haben eine freundschaftliche Vertrauensbasis. Und jetzt sag du was. Los! Komm! Na?

"Die E. lieben sich eigentlich gar nicht," schrieb das Kind ins blaue Heft. "Die E. sind miteinander befreundet. Meine Großeltern lieben sich, meine wahren Eltern lieben sich, ich liebe meine wahren Verwandten, ich liebe meine Schwester und meine Brüder." Über die Brüder, was das für welche sein könnten, müßte es noch viel nachdenken. Marlenchen, das Schwesterchen vom Photo, in der Umarmung mit ihm, dem Kind mit dem Kränzchen auf dem Kopf, war ihm ganz und gar klar. Dem Marlenchen gegenüber war das Kind nicht *Paul,* sondern Paula, aber am meisten war es beim Marlenchen das *Paulinchen.* Brüder hätte ich vielleicht gar keine. Es nahm sich vor, das demnächst zu entscheiden. Das Kind hatte keine Lust, die neuen Eltern *Liebt ihr euch* zu fragen. Es hatte halbwegs Lust, ihnen *Ihr liebt euch ja gar nicht* zu sagen. Es hatte jetzt aber am meisten Lust, wieder mit sich allein zu sein, also nichts zu sagen.

Ein bißchen unvernünftig wirds wohl gewesen sein von uns, wie wir beim ersten Mal drauf reagiert haben, als wir von deinen lieben, aber für dich doch entschieden zu alten Großeltern hörten, daß du noch immer einen Nachttopf benutzt, pardon: ein *Töpfchen,* nicht wahr?

and you must do it occasionally. Later Christa and Kurt often discussed this remark of the child. Unfortunately we probably didn't have our reaction well enough under control. *You* at least looked rather flabbergasted. *You* at least looked outraged enough.

You have made an important mistake here. *You* have unfortunately not kept your cool at all. But we took ourselves in hand again remarkably quickly. Is she a little mean at times, little Paula? What was she trying to achieve? Kurt, I dare say she meant that woman student from Erlangen. Your petting with Ernesto my dear Christa, you should be a little — well, she observes keenly, and anyhow it is completely unnecessary, the way you two always lie in each others arms and kiss each other. She also seems to read our mail. In case you should occasionally read our mail, Paula, do not be misled by some letters from admirers. There are people who care very much about what we write and so on. They feel related to us and so forth. Besides it is really not nice to read mail that is addressed to other people. Because we do not fundamentally forbid you to do anything my dear, you unfortunately, occasionally go a little too far. What is not expressly *forbidden* is not by the same token expressly *allowed,* right? What can one do. We must put up with your little misdemeanors, your little tasteless acts, for better or worse. But it would be nicer for all three of us, if you too would behave like a partner. She does not understand this word again, Kurt said to Christa. Christa said, like a pal, like our pal, that's how you should behave towards us, like we, Kurt and I have behaved towards each other for many years. We operate on the basis of a trusting friendship. And now you say something. Come on! Go! Well?

"The P.s really do not love each other at all," the child wrote in the blue exercise book. "The P.s are friends with each other. My grandparents love each other, my true parents love each other, I love my true relatives, I love my sister and my brothers." About the brothers, and what they could be like, she would still have to think a lot. Marlenchen, the little sister in the photograph, embracing her, the child with a little wreath on her head, was entirely clear to her. With regard to Marlenchen the child was not *Paul,* but Paula, but mostly she was *little Pauline* to Marlenchen. Perhaps I will not even have any brothers. She planned to make a decision about that soon. The child did not feel like asking her new parents *Do you love each other?* To an extent she felt like telling them *You do not love each other at all.* But now most of all she felt like being by herself again, that is, to say nothing.

A little unreasonable it must have been on our part, the way we reacted when we heard from your dear grandparents who are nonetheless too old for you, that you are still using a chamberpot, pardon, a *potty,* right?

Die Großeltern sind nicht zu alt, sagte das Kind. Es mußte jetzt sehr aufpassen. Wenn es jetzt nicht sehr aufpaßte, würde es sofort todunglücklich. Besser weggehen. Paula entfernte sich als *Paul*. *Paul* tat so, als lese er. Aber ganz so isoliert wollte das Kind nun doch wieder nicht bleiben, noch nicht: also nahm es sich keins von den Büchern, die Christa und Kurt nach gründlicher Beschäftigung mit der jeweils kinderpsychologisch geeigneten Lektüre ihm besorgten und die es lesen sollte. Mit einem Buch vom Stapel, der für das Kind vorgesehen war und durch den es profitieren würde, hätte man es in Ruhe gelassen. Warum mogelte es nicht so, daß es seine Ruhe hatte? Warum wollte es einen Unmut hervorrufen? Warum wollte es doch noch einmal aufgescheucht, befragt, beredet werden? Entschieden machte es doch erneut einen Annäherungsversuch, gerade indem es sich für ein Buch von der unerwünschten Sorte entschied. "Trostbüchlein der Poesie." Was willst du denn mit dem alten Schinken? Komm, laß das weg, nimm was Lustiges, Vernünftiges stattdessen. Du verstehst doch diese ganzen Gedichte überhaupt noch nicht, du brauchst auch gar nicht, außerdem ist zu viel Kitsch drin, zu viel schlechte Literatur. Laß das, Paula. Ist das ein Verbot, fragte das Kind. Es war stolz auf seine Frage. Die Frage war wirklich listig, fast heimtückisch, sie legte die Erwachsenen mit ihrem Verbotsverbot ganz saftig rein. Ach, ein Verbot – hör doch auf. *Das* natürlich ist es nicht. Es ist ein guter Rat. Wir wollen rechtzeitig deinen Sinn für Geschmack entwickeln. Ich finde die Gedichte schön, sagte das Kind. In deinem Alter machst du dir durch diese Art von Lesestoff ein falsches Bild von der Welt. Das Zeug ist aus andern Jahrhunderten. Die Leute schrieben und dachten und fühlten damals anders als wir heutigen Menschen. Sie waren noch längst nicht so weit wir wir.

Christa und Kurt saßen mit Großeltern und Kind im weinroten Wohnzimmer der Großeltern. Man kann sich hier ja kaum bewegen, so viel steht hier rum, sagte Christa leise zu Kurt. Die Großeltern waren schwerhörig. Die Großmutter schenkte Kaffee ein. Der Großvater hatte die Bemerkung vielleicht doch gehört. Bei uns ist eben sehr viel Weiträumigkeit, wir haben viel Platz, erklärte Kurt für den Fall, daß der Großvater doch etwas gehört hatte. Niemand will ja die alten Leute kränken, sagten Christa und Kurt zum Kind. Sie japst wie ein Fisch an der Angel in der Luft, dachte das Kind, das noch keinen Fisch an der Angel in der Luft gesehen hatte; aber eine Zeichnung in einem Bilderbuch mit einem unwilligen Fisch, der das Meer verlassen hatte, erinnerte das Kind an Christa zwischen den Sachen der Großeltern. Christa tat so, als bekomme sie hier keine Luft. Nicht wahr, Paula, du weißt ja, wie es bei uns ausschaut. Da kriegt man ziemlich leicht anderswo die Platzangst, ich meine, wenn man aus einem Raum wie unserem *Atelier* kommt, irgendwohin, fast egal wohin, kaum jemand, der diese Weite um sich hat. Seit wir in dem Haus mit dem großen und durch die Arbeitsempore von Kurt teilweise sogar zweistöckigen Raum wohnen, ists mir fast überall sonstwo zu eng. Sie würden das verstehen, wenn Sie es gesehen

My grandparents are not too old, the child said. She had to be very careful now. If she was not very careful now, she would immediately be deathly unhappy. Better to go away. Paul left as *Paul*. *Paul* acted as though he was reading. But that isolated the child did not want to remain either, not yet: thus she did not take one of the books that Christa and Kurt had bought after careful deliberation about reading material that would be psychologically suitable and that she should read. With a book from the pile that had been selected for the child and from which she would profit, she would have been left in peace. Why did she not cheat for the sake of peace? Why did she want to provoke anger? Why did she want to be stirred up once more, questioned, talked at?

Clearly she made a renewed attempt at communication just by choosing a book of the undesirable sort. "Little Book of Comfort Poetry." What do you want with that old hat? Come, leave that, take something amusing, sensible instead. You do not understand all those poems yet, you don't have to, besides there is too much Kitsch in it, too much bad literature. Leave that, Paula. Is this a taboo, the child asked. She was proud of her question. The question was really shrewd, almost sly. She sucked the adults in pretty well with their taboo to taboo. Heavens, a taboo — stop it. *That's* not it of course. It's good advice. We want to develop your taste early. I find the poems beautiful, the child said. At your age you get a false picture of the world through this kind of reading material. That stuff is from another century. People wrote and thought and felt differently than today's people. They were not nearly as advanced as we are.

Christa and Kurt were sitting with grandparents and child in the grandparents' wine-red living room. One can hardly move here, there is so much around, Christa said softly to Kurt. The grandparents were hard of hearing. The grandmother poured coffee. The grandfather might have heard the remark after all. We have a lot of space, there is a lot of room at our place, Kurt explained, in case the grandfather had heard something. Nobody wants to offend the two old people, Christa and Kurt said to the child. She gasps like a fish on a hook in the air, the child thought, who had never seen a fish on a hook in the air; but a drawing in a picture book, showing an unwilling fish that had left the sea, reminded the child of Christa among the grandparents' things. Christa acted as though she was not getting any air here. Not so, Paula, you know what it looks like at our place? One can rather easily get claustrophobia somewhere else, I mean if one comes from a room like our *studio* and goes anywhere else no matter where, there is hardly anybody who would find that much space around him. Ever since we have been living in this house with the large room that, because of Kurt's work hallway, partly extends over two stories, I feel closed in in almost any other place. They would

hätten. Na, vielleicht wird mal was draus, vielleicht werden wirs später mal schaffen und Sie zu einem Besuch bei uns abholen, wenn erst die kleine Paula ganz bei uns lebt, nicht wahr, Kurt? Nur, das große Handicap: Zeit haben wir eigentlich nie, das Privatleben kommt eigentlich immer ein bißchen zu kurz, weil wir beide so völlig beschlagnahmt sind von den Schreibereien. Christa lachte. Und demnächst erst recht, ich meine, da gehören alle Pausen, die wir uns fürs Private gönnen, unserer neuen kleinen Lebensgefährtin, dem Paulinchen, hm? Sie können sich fest drauf verlassen, einsam wird sie sich nicht fühlen bei uns. "Paulinchen war allein zu Haus," das wird auf *unser* Paulinchen nicht zutreffen. Das Haus ist ja außerdem sozusagen türlos, und sie hat keine Besuchssperren bei Kurt und mir und keine Zimmerverbote und nirgendwo Grenzen, sie kann uns – einen von uns, wir machen das miteinander ab – jederzeit erreichen, wenn sie uns braucht. Wir teilen uns in sie, in ihre Sorgen, sozusagen.

Von Satz zu Satz merkte das Kind, wie die Zukunft übler und übler wurde. Trotzdem hörte es ohne Angst zu. Darüber, daß die Sätze ihm zwar einen Ekel machten, aber keine Angst, wunderte es sich später oft sehr. Der Ekel war auch wie etwas Entferntes, er war eigentlich wie eine Neugier auf einen Ekel. Das Kind spürte, so lang es sich bei den Großeltern aufhielt und im weinroten Zimmer das weinrote Zimmer genoß, daß der ganze Erläuterungskram, der doch seine eigene Zukunft betraf, es noch gar nicht selber betraf. Es war ihm, als würde man es, beharrlich auf der Suche nach einem Schmerz Stück für Stück die Haut abstichelnd, zu einem Aufwachen bringen wollen, als bliebe es aber taub wie eine Backe nach dem Zahnarzt, wie eine Zunge und ein halbes Gesicht, wenn der Zahnarzt eine Injektion gemacht hatte. Nichts tat weh. Die Nachttopf-Offenbarung tat im weinroten Zimmer auch noch nicht weh, war aber etwas peinlich.

Das Kind hatte die Besuchsstunden der beiden Erwachsenen bei den Großeltern ganz gern. Die beiden Erwachsenen kamen ihm zu jung vor für ein Zusammenleben mit ihnen. Aber es fürchtete sich damals nicht vor der Zukunft. Die Zukunft war eine Geschichte in weiter Ferne, und gar nicht einmal seine eigene Geschichte, das Kind fühlte sich stark, bärenkräftig. Es selber könnte alles noch, kurz bevor es wirklich Ernst wurde, verhindern, es würde einen riesigen Widerstand veranstalten. Darauf freute es sich. Es würde alle Leute in Erstaunen setzen. Es hat diese Zeiten im Leben des Kindes gegeben, da hat es sich abgesichert gefühlt, einfach so, ganz selbstverständlich.

Gabriele Wohmann

understand if they had seen it. Well, perhaps some day it will happen, perhaps we will succeed in bringing them to us for a visit, when little Paula will be living with us for good, not so Kurt? Only one big handicap: time, we hardly ever have it, our private life is always somewhat short changed because we are both so very involved in our writing. Christa laughed. And soon even more so, I mean that all the breaks that we take for our private lives will belong to our new little companion, our little Pauline, hm? You can rest assured that she will not feel lonely with us. "Little Pauline was alone at home" that will not apply to *our* Pauline. Besides, the house is practically without doors and there are no restrictions to visits with Kurt and myself and no rooms off-limits, no boundaries anywhere, she can reach us — one of us, we will arrange that between us — at any time, whenever she needs us. We will share her, her problems so to speak.

From sentence to sentence the child noticed how the future became worse and worse. Nevertheless she listened without fear. Later she would find it amazing that those sentences nauseated her but did not frighten her. Her nausea was really like something distant, like a curiosity about nausea. The child sensed that as long as she stayed with the grandparents and in the wine-red room, enjoying the wine-red room, that the whole rubbish of explaining her own future did not touch her yet. It seemed as though someone was probing her skin piece by piece with a pin, trying to find a pain, trying to wake her up, but it was as if she remained numb like a cheek at the dentist's, like a tongue and half the face after the dentist gave an injection. Nothing hurt. Even the chamberpot-revelation did not hurt in the wine-red room, but it was slightly embarrassing.

The child enjoyed the visiting hours of the two adults as the grandparents up to a point. The two adults seemed too young for her to live with them. But at that time she was not afraid of the future. The future was a story far removed, and not even her own story, the child felt strong, strong as a bear. She herself would be able to prevent everything shortly before it became really serious. She would organize a gigantic resistance. She looked forward to that. She would amaze everyone. There were these times in the life of the child, when she felt secure, simply and wholly, as a matter of course.

Gabriele Wohmann
translated by *Janet Gluckman* and *Elizabeth Rüthschi Herrmann*

Erdschwere   *Japanese ink on paper 22.2 x 26.3 cm.*   Marion Settekorn

Hockender   *Japanese ink and graphite on paper 76 x 52 cm.*   **Marion Settekorn**

Zusammen   *Japanese ink on paper 31.5 x 22.5 cm.*   Marion Settekorn

MEINE NEUGIER

Meine Neugier, die ausgewanderte, ist zurückgekehrt.
Mit blanken Augen spaziert sie wieder
Auf der Seite des Lebens.
Salve, sagt sie, freundliches Schiefgesicht,
Zweijährige Stimme, unschuldig wie ein Veilchen,
Grünohren, Wangen wie Fischhaut, Tausendschön
Alles begrüßt sie, das Häßliche und das Schöne.

Gerade als hätte ich nicht schon längst genug,
Holt sie mir meinen Teil, meinen Löwenteil,
An dem, was geschieht, aus Häusern, die mich nichts angehen.
Ein Ohr soll ich haben für jeden Untergang
Und Augen für jede Gewalttat.

Die schönste Abendröte kommt dagegen nicht auf,
Die zartesten Gräser sind machtlos.
Wie sehne ich mich nach der Zeit, als sie nichts zu bestimmen hatte,
Als ich hintrieb ruhig im Kielwasser des Todes,
In den milchigen Strudeln der Träume.

Vergeblich jag ich sie fort, meine Peinigerin.
Da ist sie wieder, trottet und hüpft,
Streift mich mit ihrem heißen Hündinnenatem.

Vergeblich beklage ich mich.
Was für ein schreckliches Lärmen,
Was für ein Gelauf und Geläute,
Was für eine Stimme, die aus mir selber kommt,
Spottdrosselstimme, und sagt,
Was willst du, du lebst.

Marie Luise Kaschnitz

MY CURIOSITY

My curiosity, the emigrant, has returned.
With shining eyes she strolls again
On the side of life.
Hail!, she says, friendly old sour-face,
Two-year old's voice, innocent as a violet,
Green-ears, cheeks like fish-skin, daisies
She greets everything, the ugly and the beautiful.

Just as if I hadn't long ago had enough,
She secures for me my share, my lion's share
Of that which occurs, from houses which do not concern me.
I should have an ear for every collapse
And eyes for every act of violence.

The loveliest sunset red is no match for those,
The tenderest grasses are powerless.
How I long for the time when she had no part to play,
When I trod along quietly in the wake of death,
In the milky whirlpools of dreams.

In vain I chase her away, my torturess.
Here she is again, she trots and leaps,
Brushes against me with her hot hound's breath.

In vain I complain.
What a terrible uproar,
What a bustle and baying,
What a voice, that comes from me,
Mockingbird's voice, and says,
What do you want, you're alive.

Marie Luise Kaschnitz
translated by *Sally Robertson*

143

FÖRHOPPNING

Jag vill vara ogenerad —
därför struntar jag i ädla stilar,
ärmarna kavlar jag upp.
Diktens deg jäser . . .
O en sorg —
att ej kunna baka katedraler . . .
Formernas höghet —
trägna längtans mål.
Nutidens barn —
har din ande ej sitt rätta skal?
Innan jag dör
bakar jag en katedral.

Edith Södergran

HOPE

I don't want to be constrained —
that is why I could care less about noble styles,
I roll up my sleeves.
The dough of poetry rises . . .
Oh the grief —
not to be able to bake cathedrals . . .
Exalted forms —
what one strives so intensely to achieve.
Modern child —
can't you find a proper skin for your spirit?
Before I die
I'll bake a cathedral.

Edith Södergran
translated by *Christer L. Mossberg*

DINGGEDICHT

Ich bekam zum Auszug
dennoch
eine Vase geschenkt.

Das Notizbuch kauften wir
auf der Insel
in dem einzigen Laden.

Den gestreiften Kiesel
hast du gefunden
in der Bucht Aber-Bach in Wales.

Mit diesem Tintenstift
schrieb ich,
was niemand mochte, ich auch nicht.

Bitte.
Machen Sie die Geschichtenabdrücke weg,
und außerdem hätte ich gern
ein paar Gegenstände mit Eigen-
schaften.

Petra von Morstein

THING POEM

Moving out
I was given
a vase.

The notebook was bought
on the island
in the one store there.

You found
the striped pebble
on the beach at Aber-Bach, in Wales.

With this pencil
I wrote
things nobody liked, not even I.

Please.
Take off these story tags.
I'd really like
a few things with
qualities of their own.

Petra von Morstein
translated by *Rosmarie Waldrop*

* * *

te słowa istniały zawsze
w otwartym uśmiechu słonecznika
w ciemnym skrzydle wrony
i jeszcze
we framudze przymkniętych drzwi

nawet gdy drzwi nie było
istniały
w gałęziach prostego drzewa

a ty chcesz
żebym je miała na własność
żebym była
skrzydłem wrony brzozą i latem
chcesz
żebym dźwięczała
brzękiem uli otwartych na słońce

głupcze
ja nie mam tych słów
pożyczam
od wiatru od pszczół i od słońca

Halina Poswiatowska

* * *

these words have always existed
in the sunflower's broad smile
the crow's black wing
and in the frame of a door left ajar

even when the door was not there
they existed
in the branches of any ordinary tree

but you want me
to take them
to be
the crow's wing the birch the summer
you want me to drone
like a beehive open to the sun

you fool
I don't have these words
I only borrow
from the wind the bee the sun

Halina Poswiatowska
translated by *Grazýna Drabik* and *Sharon Olds*

I D'aquelas que cantan as pombas y as frores
   todos din que teñen alma de muller,
   pois eu que n' as canto. Virxe d' a Paloma,
   ¡Ay!, ¿de qué a teréi?

II Ben sei que non hay nada
    novo en baixo d' o ceo,
    qu' antes outros pensaron
    as cousas qu' hora eu penso.

    E ben ¿para qu' excribo?
    E ben, porqu' así somos,
    relox que repetimos
    eternamente o mesmo

III Tal com' as nubes
     que leva ò vento,
     y agora asombran, y agora alegran
     os espaços inmensos d' o ceo,
     así as ideas
     loucas qu' eu teño.
     as imaxes de múltiples formas
     extrañas feituras, de cores incertos,
     agora asombran,
     agora acraran,
     o fo do sin fondo d'o meu pensamento.

     Rosalía de Castro

150

I   Those that sing of the doves and the flowers
all say they have the soul of a woman,
And I who don't sing, Virgin of the Dove,
what can my soul be?

II   I know well that there is nothing new
under the sun,
that what I am thinking now
was thought before.

Well, then, why do I write?
Because this is the way we are,
like a clock, we repeat ourselves,
eternally the same.

III   Like clouds,
clouds that are lifted by the wind,
first they're somber, and then they show
immense spaces of blue sky,
just like the crazy ideas
I have.
These images take on many strange forms,
many strange forms and vague colors —
colors that now darken
now brighten
the endless depths of my thought.

Rosalía de Castro
translated by *Marian Moore*

VOY A DORMIR

Dientes de flores, cofia de rocío,
manos de hierbas, tú, nodriza fina,
tenme prestas las sábanas terrosas
y el edredón de musgos encardados.

Voy a dormir, nodriza mía, acuéstame.
Ponme una lámpara a la cabecera;
una constelación; la que te guste;
todas son buenas; bájala un poquito.

Déjame sola: oyes romper los brotes…
te acuna un pie celeste desde arriba
y un pájaro te traza unos compases

para que olvides…Gracias. Ah, un encargo:
si él llama nuevamente por teléfono
le dices que no insista, que he salido…

Alfonsina Storni

A UN JILGUERO

Cítara de carmín que amaneciste
trinando endechas a tu amada esposa
y paciéndole el ámbar a la rosa
el pico de oro de coral teñiste.

Dulce jilguero, pajarillo triste,
que apenas el aurora viste hermosa,
cuando al tono primero de una glosa
la muerte hallaste y el compás perdiste.

No hay en la vida, no, segura muerte;
tu misma voz al cazador convida,
para que el golpe cuando tira acierte.

¡Oh fortuna buscada, aunque temida!
¿Quién pensara que cómplice en tu muerte
fuera, por no callar, tu propia vida?

Sor Juana Inés De La Cruz

I'M GOING TO SLEEP

Teeth of flowers, hair net of dew,
hands of herbs, you, gentle nurse,
have ready for me the earthy sheets
and the quilt of carded moss.

I'm going to sleep, my nurse, put me to bed.
Put a lamp at the bedside;
a constellation; whichever one you like;
they're all good, turn it down a little.

Leave me alone: you hear the sprouts break forth. . .
a celestial foot rocks you from above
and a bird traces rhythms for you

so you'll forget. . . Thank you. Ah, a request:
if he calls again on the telephone
tell him not to insist, that I've gone out. . .

Alfonsina Storni
Translated by *Janice G. Titiev*

TO A GOLDFINCH

Zither of rouge, you sang at early sun rise,
laments for your beloved wife
and grazing the amber of the rose
tinted your golden beak coral.

Sweet goldfinch, sad paper kite,
you no sooner saw the beautiful dawn
then at the tune's first note
you found death and lost the song.

There is in this life no best time for death;
your own voice invites the hunter,
and guides the shot he fires to its target.

Oh fortune that man seeks and yet fears!
Who would think your life, that unsilenced
song, would be death's own accomplice?

Sor Juana Inés de la Cruz
translated by *Pamela Uschuk*

KRIM

Die brennenden Bäume bei Jalta.
Die heisse Fremde die Krim.
Die ungeheure Bläue.
Und ich verstummt.
Im Traum in trüben Tagen
Zu Haus, die fallen bald,
Will ich die Sprache austräumen,
In der man spricht mit Bäumen,
Die *brennen*. Da helfen nicht Worte wie
Wald.

Eva Strittmatter

POETIK

Immer die alten Worte:
Wolke, Wasser und Wind,
Wege, bewohnbare Orte,
Haus und vor allem: das Kind.
Immer die Elemente:
Zeugung, Geburt und Tod.
Was uns von anderen trennte:
Das ist gemeinsame Not.
Immer das nackte Leben
Hinter dem schönen Schein.
Und versuch ich auch, mich zu erheben:
Die Erde holt mich doch ein.

Eva Strittmatter

CRIMEA

The burning trees at Yalta.
The hot   strange land, the Crimea.
The immense blue.
Myself, silenced.
In dreams, in the dreary days
At home, how soon they pass,
I want to finish the dream of a language
Where one speaks with trees that *burn*.
There's no help then in words like
Woods.

Eva Strittmatter
translated by *Hanna Mosquera*

POETICS

Always the ancient words:
Clouds, water and wind,
Paths, livable places,
House, and especially: child.
Always the basic elements:
Begetting, birth and death.
The separation from others:
That is the common affliction.
Always the naked existence
Beneath the fair facade.
And though I try to raise myself:
The earth still overtakes me.

Eva Strittmatter
Translated by *Hanna Mosquera*

ZIKADENNAECHTE

Zikadennächte. Man sollte sie
Auf *einem* Ton nachsingen.
Wie soll man die Anti-Melodie
Der Zikaden in Worte zwingen?
Die Wärme der Steine. Der graue Geruch
Und das Flüstern der Gräser im Finstern.
Verkrüppelte Kiefern am Felsenabbruch.
Und hinter Wermut und Ginstern
Der südliche See, der *da* ist und schweigt,
Ueberschrillt von den Zikaden:
Ein irr gewordener Geiger geigt
Auf einem Silberfaden.

Eva Strittmatter

156

CICADA NIGHTS

Cicada nights. A *single* note
Is needed to intone them.
Cicada's anti-melody,
How force it into words?
The warm stones, the grey odor,
The whisper of grass in the dark.
Twisted pines by the rock fall.
Behind wormwood and broom
The southern lake, that is *there* and silent,
Outshrilled by the cicadas:
A maddened fiddler strumming
A single silver string.

Eva Strittmatter
translated by *Hanna Mosquera*

Natasa Sotiropoulos

oil on canvas 48" x 60"

Kaldis Monologue

Natasa Sotiropoulos

oil on canvas 48" x 60"

Conversations with Domenikos

DABEI

Einer spricht
über etwas und
viele hören zu und
ich höre zu wahrscheinlich
wäre jedes Wort
dasselbe
mein Platz wäre leer oder
irgendein Platz der nicht
leer ist wäre leer und
jemand
säße auf meinem Platz
wenn ich nicht
dabei wäre.

Auf einem zentralen Bahnhof
habe ich
noch weniger Einfluß.
Immerhin
bin ich ein Unterschied.

Petra von Morstein

PRESENT

Somebody talks
about something and
many listen and
I listen probably
every word would be
the same
if my seat were empty or
if some seat which is not
empty were empty and
somebody
sat in my seat
if I were not
present.

In a big station
I have
even less influence.
Even so
I make a difference.

Petra von Morstein
translated by *Rosmarie Waldrop*

IM FALLE VON HUMMERN

Es gibt
2 Arten die einen tun
lebendige Hummer
in kochendes
Wasser des Aromas
wegen
man kann dann aber
Schmerzensschreie wenn man
im Falle von Hummern
von Schmerzen überhaupt
sprechen kann mikrofonisch
wahrnehmen

Die andern
aus humanitären Gründen
in kaltes
vor dem Kochen.

Petra von Morstein

IN THE CASE OF LOBSTERS

There are
2 methods some put
the live lobster
in boiling
water for the best
taste
but
with a microphone
you can hear screams
of pain if
in the case of lobsters
one can speak of such a thing
as pain

Others
for humanitarian reasons
put it in cold
then bring to the boil

Petra von Morstein
translated by *Rosmarie Waldrop*

Un manso río, una vereda estrecha,
un campo solitario y un pinar,
y el viejo puente, rústico y sencillo,
completando tan grata soledad.

¿Qué es soledad? Para llenar el mundo
basta a veces un solo pensamiento,
Por eso hoy, hartos de belleza, encuentras
el puente, el río, y el pinar desiertos.

No son nube ni flor los que enamoran,
eres tú, corazón, triste o dichoso,
ya del dolor y del placer el árbitro,
quien seca el mar y hace habitable el polo.

Rosalía de Castro

A tame river, a narrow path,
A lonely field and a cluster of pines;
The old bridge, rustic and simple.
A portrait of solitude.

Solitude? To fill the world at times
It takes but a single thought.
So today you look at this graceful scene,
The bridge, the river, the pines,
And find it homely.

It isn't clouds, it isn't flowers that inspire.
It is the heart, grieving or rejoicing,
That is the arbiter of pain or pleasure,
That dries the sea and makes habitable the pole.

Rosalía de Castro
translated by *Barbara Dale May*

臨江仙　戊子（卅八年）歲暮初抵嶺南　祁

李

十載歸來仍故我　戰墟滿目塵埃　可能劫外認餘灰

堂深留夢永　寒重撥絃哀　初日園林桃杏淺

有人曾共徘徊　春風入鬢可眉開　而今成往事

嗚咽逐秦淮。

北去南來多少路　嶺雲黯黯長橫　山溫地暖

且消停　幽花堪摘　薄醉最宜醒　天末微波

分海色　潮來頃刻都青　莫從過去問來程

湖山驚鷲昨夢　風雨感蒼生。

Calligraphy by Yang Toa-Ping

ON ARRIVING AT LING-NAN, JANUARY, 1949
Two tz'u to the tune of Lin-chiang Hsien "The Immortal by the River"

1. Ten years gone.
        I am still the same.
   The dust of the battlefield
        is all I see.
   Was anything left behind
        in the ash?
   A manor can hold its dreams forever
   But in this dull cold
        the strings would wail.

   Sunrise over parks
        of blooming peach trees:
   Someone walked here
        with me once.
   Spring winds fill
        and freshen my face.
   All that is now the past:
   A noise
        chasing the Ch'in-huai River.

2. North to south I travel.
        How far have I come?
   Dark clouds cover
        the mountain range.
   Below, the soil is warm.
   I'll stay a while.
   When I am lonely,
        I pick lonely flowers.
   When I drink just a bit,
        I stay awake longer.

   At sky's end, tiny waves
        split the sea.
   The tide comes in
        and the world is blue.
   Don't ask the past
        where you are going.
   Lakes and mountains
        frightened my dreams last night.
   Now wind and rain move me
        closer to all people.

   Li Chi
   translated by *Li Chi*
            and Michael O'Connor

LE VIDE

Je descendais, je m'accrochais à des broussailles
Cherchant quelque rocher pour assurer mes pas.
D'habitude nous avons en nous ce compas
Qui mesure vite une pente à notre taille.
On sait s'il faut continuer une voltige
Et même si le goufre est un peu en retrait.
Mais ici plusieurs fois de suite le vertige
Du vide ine laissait imaginer après
La même chute encore.

Edith Boissonnas

INITIALES

Des oiseaux blancs dessous noir dessus
S'espaçaient se délivraient de lentes dédicaces
Écrites sur les branches de l'arbre défendu,
Très haut ne laissant plus aucune trace.
Tantôt cachés tantôt perçus, puis opposés
Leur jeu suivait le réseau redoutable
Du végétal divin, où nul n'avait osé
Chercher son fruit, plus mûr, plus délectable.

Edith Boissonnas

LE VIDE

Falling, I grabbed onto some bushes,
Looking for a crag to curb my descent.
We have in us naturally this scale
Which weighs our leanings against our skills.
We know when to follow through with a leap
Or if the gulf is perhaps too wide.
But here, repeatedly, vertigo
From the abyss left me an after-image
Of that same fall, time upon time.

Edith Boissonnas
Translated by *Beth Bentley*

INITIALS

Some birds white below, black above,
Space themselves delivered of slow dedications
Written on the branches of the forbidden tree
Very high, leaving no trace.
Sometimes hidden, sometimes seen, then changing places,
Their play follows the dangerous structure
Of divine vegetation where none has dared
Search for the riper, more delectable fruit.

Edith Boissonnas
Translated by *Beth Bentley*

LES TÉMOINS

De ce passé chargé émergent leurs visages.
Ils se rapprochent s'éloignent indifférents
Aux cris du nouveau venu aux vieux outrages.
Ils songent lucides que rien n'est différent.
Lentement dans les couloirs ils se promènent
Et ne s'étonnent pas des chocs des éclairs
Étincelants lorsqu'une porte s'ouvre vaine.
Ils savent bien qu'il vaut toujours mieux se taire.
C'est à peine s'ils découvrent un peu leurs gencives.
Ce n'est pas un sourire, aucun étonnement,
Rien ne peut déranger l'amère perspective.
On n'inventera plus aucun raffinement.
Ah le nouveau venu traqué dans ces mensonges,
Il aimait ces détours, s'avançait curieux,
Il sent se refermer une ombre qui le ronge
Sans défense devant des regards aussi vieux.

Edith Boissonnas

THE WITNESSES

From the charged past their faces emerge.
They approach, back off, indifferent
To cries of the new come to old outrages.
They dream, certain that nothing changes.
Slowly in the corridors they stroll
Unastonished at the lightning shock
That glitters when a door opens uselessly.
They know well it's best to be silent;
They scarcely uncover their gums.
Not a smile, no amazement,
Nothing can change the bitter prospect.
No more refinements will be invented.
Ah, the new came trapped in lies.
It loved the turnings, advancing curious.
Defenceless before those old old stares.
It feels the gnawing shadow closing in.

Edith Boissonnas
translated by *Beth Bentley*

JEMAND SCHWEIGT

JEMAND SCHWEIGT
und du glaubst er spricht
und du antwortest
und sprichst gut
und entblößt dich
haut um haut die du nicht
geben kannst du der du sprichst
und es wird kalt und kälter

jemand schweigt
und du wartest
auf das schweigen
nach allen enden
und weiter hinaus
und es trägt nicht das wort
und nicht weißt du
wo das licht ist
das helle und dunkle

jemand geht
und du glaubst
er geht gut
und du folgst ihm
und haltst seinen schritt aus
und wirst nicht irre

jemand geht
und du glaubst er geht weich
auf weichen sohlen
und du pflückst das weiche
und läht das harte stehen
und das eis knirscht
und du sagst ich hör es nicht

Elisabeth Borchers

174

SOMEONE IS SILENT

Someone Is Silent
and you believe he speaks
and you answer
and speak well
and bare yourself
skin by skin which can't be
given you who speak
in the familiar
it is getting cold and colder

someone is silent
and you wait
for the silence
after all ending
and beyond
but it does not carry the word
not to where
the light is you know
the bright and dark

someone goes
and you believe
he goes well
and you follow him
and tolerate his step
and don't go astray

someone goes
and you believe he goes softly
on soft soles
and you pluck the soft
and leave the hard behind
and ice crunches
and you say I don't hear it

Elisabeth Borchers
translated by *Gudrun Mouw*

IMMER EIN ANDERES

und du willst auferstehen lebenslang
und der vogel beschattet das haus noch
im tode und der wind pflanzt sich fort
in den tag in die nacht und schüttelt
dein aug aber es ist leer auch die
papierkörbe sind leer und die leere
ist eingeschlafen und weckt dich nicht mehr

weh dir die luft ist leer sie nimmt dich
nicht der baum ist leer er nimmt dich
nicht kein vogel bist du vogel mehr kein
stein der weint um dich mein stein und
auch die sonne nicht und nicht der mond

und du willst auferstehen lebenslang
und fragst und fragst die nächste stadt
die andre stadt und klopfst und fragst
ist dies die nächste stadt das nächste
haus das haus ist leer die kerzen die
da brennen brennen nicht so lösch sie
aus es weckt dich niemand niemals mehr

Elisabeth Borchers

ALWAYS SOMETHING ELSE

and you want to rise from the dead all your life
and the bird still shadows the house
in death and the wind plants itself
into the day the night and shakes
your eye but it is empty the wastebaskets
are also empty and the emptiness
has fallen asleep and doesn't wake you anymore

woe the air is empty and doesn't take you
the tree is empty and doesn't take you
you are no bird you looney moreover no
stone which cries for you my stone and
also not the sun and not the moon

and you want to rise from the dead all your life
and ask and ask the next city
another city and knock and ask
is this the next city the next
house the house is empty the candles
that burn there don't burn so extinguish them
no one will ever wake you again

Elisabeth Borchers
translated by *Gudrun Mouw*

LES MOINEAUX FONT GLISSER...

Les moineaux font glisser les dépêches sur les fils élec-triques. Loin des rails, le train repose sans roues. Les épouvantails, souvent par couples, se gonflent de vents, de fumée de charbon et surtout de la substance même du crépuscule. Inutile de chercher à reconnaitre le bord du chapeau dont ils sont coiffés ou de crier mer-veille qu'un manche à balai danse une sarabande. Même les moineaux s'abstiennent de picoter et de pépier. Dorénavant les fils électriques serviront de cadre pro-tectéur contre l'invasion tenace de l'infini. C'est le jour où leurs mailles se lieront au filigrane solaire que l'on nous dira tout.

Renée Riese Hubert

The sparrows hurry the telegrams over the electric wires.
Far from the rails, the train without wheels takes its rest.
Scarecrows, often by twos, blow themselves up with the wind,
soot, and above all with the very substance of dusk. What
good does it do to recognize the brim of the hat they are
wearing or to get ecstatic when a broomstick dances a
sarabanda. Even the sparrow refrains from picking and peeping.
In the future the electric wires will serve as a frame
against the tenacious invasion of the infinite. On the day
when their net will link up with the solar filigree, we shall
know the truth.

Renée Riese Hubert

Dolls with the Woman   *black designer's gouache 20 x 15 cm.*   Graça Martins

Sound Sleep   *black designer's gouache 15 x 21 cm.*   Graça Martins

Black Birds *black designer's gouache 15 x 21 cm* Graça Martins

184

LIVET

Jag, min egen fånge, sägar så:
livet är icke våren, klädd i ljusgrön sammet,
eller en smekning, den man sällan får,
livet är icke ett beslut att gå
eller två vita armar, som hålla en kvar.
Livet är den trånga ringen som håller oss fången,
den osynliga kretsen, vi aldrig överträda,
livet är den nära lyckan som går oss förbi,
och tusende steg vi icke förmå oss att göra.
Livet är att förakta sig själv
och ligga orörlig på bottnen av en brunn
och veta att solen skiner däruppe
och gyllene fåglar flyga genom luften
och de pilsnabba dagarna skjuta förbi.
Livet är att vinka ett kort farväl och gå hem och sova . . .
Livet är att vara en främling för sig själv
och en ny mask för varje annan som kommer.
Livet är att handskas vårdslöst med sin egen lycka
och att stöta bort det enda ögonblicket,
livet är att tro sig vara svag och icke våga.

Edith Södergran

LIFE

I, my own prisoner, say this:
life is not spring dressed in light-green velvet,
or a caress that one seldom gets,
life is not a decision to go
or two white arms to keep one from going.
Life is the narrow circle that holds us prisoner,
the invisible ring we never break through,
life is the imminent happiness which passes us by,
and the thousand steps we are not capable of taking.
Life is to despise oneself
and lie motionless at the bottom of a well
and know that high above the sun shines
and golden birds fly
and arrow-swift days shoot by.
Life is to wave a short farewell and go home and sleep . . .
Life is to be a stranger to oneself
and a new mask for each person one meets.
Life is to deal carelessly with one's own happiness
and to push away that solitary moment,
life is to believe one is weak and does not dare.

Edith Södergran
translated by *Christer L. Mossberg*

A SEQUENCE OF DYING

1. The shock is always
    not the colour of death
    in her face when she walks,

    but to see her
    curled small in the bed
    vulnerably fetal

    and to have no
    protective womb for her.

2. This fragility. . .
    white cranes laced
    into the air

    and the sunshine
    insubstantiating city walls
    above the brief jewelled
    primulas, the tree tracery.

    a clarity of porcelain
    where brittle, temporary,
    I walk with the solidity
    of your finiteness, your pain.

3. The path
    turns upwards from her house
    that is dry shrinking itself
    stilled of multiplicity
    in rooms to a bed,
    a gown, the pink roses.

    I follow

    glad of the grass seed head
    dipped under rain
    glass droplet delicate,

    glad of the green of autumn
    the resurgence emerald
    weed warm,

beaded flax blade
and the red wild strawberry
flagrant at path edge—

emerge to earth odours
opening
under tree dripping
to the juicing, the colouring,
the glittering, the manifold,
the moving.

4. Betrayal
    It was all
    all right —

    the chapel of glowing wood
    the smallness —
    the sun in gentleness
    embalming.

    No one could dispute
    the end of an allotted life,
    not the warm bathing
    water words
    the reassuring — flannel—
    knelt gently — wiping
    with love, my children
    turn your faces
    I tender the tear,

    Not these words
    not listened to
    intoned over and folding unto —

    but the sharp looking
    direct at the casket
    and hand failure
    to touch the wood.

Helen Jacobs

ENCARGO

Cuando yo muera dadme la muerte que me falta
y no me recordéis.
No repitáis mi nombre hasta que el aire sea
transparente otra vez.

No erijáis monumentos que el espacio que tuve
entero lo devuelvo a su dueño y señor
para que advenga el otro, el esperado
y resplandezca el signo del favor.

Rosario Castellanos

HUMILDAD

Yo he sido aquélla que paseó orgullosa
El oro falso de unas cuantas rimas
Sobre su espalda, y creyó gloriosa,
De cosechas opimas.

Ten pacienca, mujer que eres oscura:
Algún día, la Forma Destructora
Que todo lo devora,
Borrará mi figura.

Se bajará a mis libros, ya amarillos,
Y alzándola en sus dedos, los carrillos
Ligeramente inflados, con un modo

De gran señor a quien lo aburre todo,
De un cansado soplido
Me aventará al olvido.

Alfonsina Storni

190

COMMISSION

When I die give me the death I lack
and don't recall me.
Don't repeat my name until the air
is transparent once again.

Don't erect monuments because the space I had
I return whole to its owner and lord
so that the other may come, the expected one,
displaying all the signs of favor.

Rosario Castellanos
translated by *Carolyne Wright*

HUMILITY

I was she who walked proud,
The false gold of a few rhymes
Across her shoulders,
and thought herself glorious,
Of rich harvests.

Be patient, woman, for you are obscure:
One day, the Destructive Form
Who devours all
Will erase my figure.

He will descend to my yellowed books,
And lifting me in his fingers,
His cheeks slightly inflated
In the manner of a haughty lord

Who is bored with everything,
With a tired puff
He will blow me into oblivion.

Alfonsina Storni
translated by *Almitra David*

Ils ont inventé l'âme afin que l'on abaisse
Le corps, unique lieu de rêve et de raison,
Asile du désir, de l'image et des sons,
Et par qui tout est mort dès le moment qu'il cesse.

Ils nous imposent l'âme, afin que lachement
On détourne les yeux du sol, et qu'on oublie,
Après l'injurieux ensevelissement,
Que sous le vin vivant tout est funèbre lie.
– Je ne commettrai pas envers votre bonté,
Envers votre grandeur, secrète mais charnelle,
O corps désagrégés, ô confuses prunelles,
La trahison de croire à votre éternité.
Je refuse l'espoir, l'altitude, les ailes,
Mais étrangère au monde et souhaitant le froid
De vos affreux tombeaux, trop bas et trop étroits,
J'affirme, en recherchant vos nuits vastes et vaines,
Qu'il n'est rien qui survive à la chaleur des veines!

Anna de Noailles

They invented the soul to abase
the body, sole space of dream and reason,
home of desire, the sound spoken, the image seen,
by which all dies at the moment of its ceasing.

They imposed the soul on us to make us cowards
who turn our eyes away from solid ground, who forget,
after the insulting injury of Christian burial,
that beneath the wine's vitality all is dregs.
— I will commit no sin against your goodness,
your greatness, secret, splendid, carnal,
o bodies now disintegrated, once-clear eyes,
I refuse the treason of believing you immortal.
I refuse hope of heaven, angel's wings,
But stranger as I am to this world, and eager for the cold
of your terrible tombs, too narrow and too low,
I still affirm, even in seeking your vast and empty dark,
that nothing lives beyond the blood's last spark!

Anna de Noailles
translated by *Kittye Delle Robbins*

INTERVIEW

Wenn er kommt, der Besucher,
Der Neugierige und dich fragt,
Dann bekenne ihm, daß du keine Briefmarken sammelst,
Keine farbigen Aufnahmen machst,
Keine Kakteen züchtest.
Daß du kein Haus hast,
Keinen Fernsehapparat,
Keine Zimmerlinde.
Daß du nicht weißt,
Warum du dich hinsetzt und schreibst,
Unwillig, weil es dir kein Vergnügen macht.
Daß du den Sinn deines Lebens immer noch nicht
Herausgefunden hast, obwohl du schon alt bist.
Daß du geliebt hast, aber unzureichend,
Daß du gekämpft hast, aber mit zaghaften Armen.
Daß du an vielen Orten zuhause warst,
Aber ein Heimatrecht hast an keinem.
Daß du dich nach dem Tode sehnst und ihn fürchtest.
Daß du kein Beispiel geben kannst als dieses:
Immer noch offen.

Marie Luise Kaschnitz

INTERVIEW

When he comes, the visitor,
The inquisitive one, and asks you,
Confess to him then that you don't collect postage stamps,
Don't take color photographs,
Don't raise cacti.
That you have no house,
No television set,
No lime tree in the living room.
That you don't know
Why you sit down and write,
Reluctantly, since it brings you no pleasure.
That you still have not discovered
The purpose of your life, although you are old.
That you have loved, but not enough,
That you have fought, but with timorous arms.
That you were at home in many places,
But are a native of none.
That you long for death and fear it.
That you can set no example but this one:
Still open.

Marie Luise Kaschnitz
translated by *Sally Robertson*

CONTRIBUTORS

ANNA AKHMATOVA, born near Odessa in 1889, spent much of her childhood in Tsarskoe Selo. In 1910 Akhmatova married Nikolai Gumilev, critic and poet, and together with Osip Mandelstam they formed the Acmeist Movement. Akhmatova's first book of poems, *Evening,* was published in 1912, her second, *Rosary,* in 1913. She died in 1966, having written seven books of poetry, some of them still unpublished in the Soviet Union. JUDITH HEMSCHEMEYER teaches creative writing at Douglass College. Her first books, *I Remember the Room was Filled with Light,* and *Very Close and Very Slow,* were published by Wesleyan University Press in 1973 and 1975. ANNA WILKINSON lives in Santa Barbara, teaching English, writing and translating. She has studied at the University of Wisconsin, where she and Judith Hemschemeyer first became friends and collaborators in literature.

CLARIBEL ALEGRÍA, poet and novelist, was born in Nicaragua in 1924, grew up in El Salvador and lives in Mallorca. Since 1955 she has published six books of poetry. *I Survive* was co-winner of the Casa de las Americas poetry prize in 1978. ELECTA ARENAL is a feminist writer, translator and activist. Associate professor of Spanish and Women's Studies, she recently composed a play drawn from the work of Anne Bradstreet and Sor Juana Inés de la Cruz. MARSHA GABRIELA DREYER grew up near Washington, D.C., and now lives in Puerto Rico. She graduated summa cum laude in economics and Latin America Studies from the University of Massachusetts-Boston in 1979 and is involved in Latin American solidarity work.

NATALIE CLIFFORD BARNEY (1876-1972) who grew in Cincinnati, Ohio, made France her adopted country. Her first book, *A Few Portrait-Sonnets of Women,* appeared in 1910, *Poems et Poèmes* and *Other Alliances* in 1921, and *Thoughts of an Amazon* in 1939. She published a volume of memoirs and short maxims under the title *Souvenirs Indiscrets* in 1960. PAULINE NEWMAN-GORDON, a professor of French at Stanford University, holds degrees from Hunter College, Columbia University and the Sorbonne, and is a member of the editorial board of the *Stanford French Review.* She has published many books, including *Corbiére, Laforgue and Apollinaire or Laughter in Tears,* 1957.

GIOCONDA BELLI (b. Managua, Nicaragua, 1948), won the University of Nicaragua poetry prize in 1972 and in 1974 published her first book of poems. She lived in exile in Costa Rica from 1975 until the Sandanista victory in July 1979. *Line of Fire* was co-winner of the Casa de las Americas poetry prize in 1978. Translators, ARENAL and DREYER. (See Alegría)

ZULEYKA BENITEZ, born in the Panama Canal Zone, grew up in Europe, Central America and the United States. She is an assistant professor at Iowa State University and is currently finishing a volume of narrative drawings to be published soon by Lost Roads Publishers.

SUJATA P. BHATT, born in Ahmedabed, India in 1956, arrived in the United States in 1968. She is a recent graduate of Goucher College where she won the Lizette Woodward Creative Writing Award and first prize in poetry in the *Preface* Creative Writing Contest.

JOAN BOISCLAIR is a poet and freelance writer living in Berkeley, California. She studied political science and literature at Swarthmore College and the University of Oregon. Her poetry has appeared in *Birthstone* and the *Tunnel Road Anthology.*

EDITH BOISSONAS, born in Switzerland and educated in France, is a regular contributor to NRF. Her books include *Demeures,* 1950; *Le Grand Jour,* 1955; *Passione,* 1958; *Limbe,* 1959; *L'Embellie,* 1966; and *Initiales,* 1971. BETH BENTLEY has published two collections of her own poetry, *Phone Calls from the Dead,* 1971; and *Country of Resemblances,* 1976; both at Ohio University Press. She is editor of *The Selected Works of Hazel Hall,* 1980, Ahasahta Press, and is the recipient of an NEA writer's grant.

ELISABETH BORCHERS, born in Homberg am Rhein, Germany, in 1946, won the Roswitha von Gandersheim Medaille with her latest collection, *Gedichte,* 1976. Her books *Gedichte,* 1961 and *Der Tisch an dem wir setzen,* 1967, are praised highly by German critics. GUDRUN MOUW's poetry and

translations have appeared or are scheduled to appear in *Cambric Poetry Project One, Cimarron Review, Blue Buildings, Bitterroot, Calliope,* and others.

ROSARIO CASTELLANOS (1925-1975), one of Mexico's foremost writers and women of letters, was the Mexican cultural ambassador to Israel at the time of her death. Her books of poetry include *Lívida Luz, De La Vigilia Estéril, Al Pie de le Letra, Trayectoria del Polvo,* and *Ciudad Real.* She has also published a collection of short stories and a novel. MAUREEN AHERN, author of several anthologies of Peruvian poetry, was co-editor of *Haravec,* a bilingual journal from Peru. Her translations appear in recent issues of *Translation, 13th Moon, The Latin American Literary Review* and others. CAROLINE WRIGHT received a Fullbright-Hays grant to Chile in 1971-72. Translations have appeared in *American Poetry Review, Hampden-Sydney Poetry Review, San Marcos Review, Malahat Review, Light,* and others. Her first book of poems, *Stealing the Children,* was published in 1978 by Ahsahta Press.

ROSALÍA DE CASTRO, one of Spain's foremost Romantic writers and poet laureate of Galicia, was born in 1837. The daughter of a young unmarried woman and a priest, she left her native Galicia at an early age to seek her literary fortune in Madrid. She lived to see two of her seven children die in childhood; was ill much of her life. She died at the age of 48 of uterine cancer. BARBARA DALE MAY teaches Spanish language and literature at the University of Oregon. She has published numerous articles in *Cuadernos Hispano-Americanos, Estudios Ibero-Americanos, Sin Nombre, The Modern Language Journal,* and is the author of *El Dilema de la Nostalgia en la Poesía de Rafael Alberti.* MARIAN MOORE, holds an MFA in translation from the University of Arkansas, has worked from Spanish, French, and Galician. Despite partial paralysis, she has studied in Spain, and translated two volumes of Galician poetry.

DAINA DAGNIJA is the recipient of a 1980 New Jersey Council on the Arts Fellowship in painting. She has had solo shows in New York, Detroit and New Jersey. Her work has been documented and videotaped by *Art/Doc/N.Y.* and is represented in the collections of Bergen Community Museum and New York City Community College. She was born in Latvia and presently resides in New Jersey.

RENÉE HUBERT, a former Guggenheim fellow, teaches French and Comparative Literature at the University of California, Irvine. She has published seven volumes of poetry in France, including *La Cité borgne, Plumes et pinceaux,* and *Chant funèbres.* Her essays on poetry and art have been widely published in the United States and France.

HELEN JACOBS, mother of two grown children, began writing four years ago. She belonged to a women's political lobbying group for some years and is now involved in local politics, community work and environmental issues in New Zealand.

SOR JUANA INÉS DE LA CRUZ (1651-1695), the greatest poet of the Spanish Colonial Period, lived in Mexico where she was reknowned for her brains and beauty at the Viceroy's court. Disillusioned with love, she became a nun and continued, through her poetry, to express her belief in women's rights. Her play, *The Divine Narcissus,* was declared heretical and, in 1691 she was censured by the church for her stands on women. She died in the Plague of 1695. PAMELA USCHUCK, a finalist in the Pablo Neruda Contest, has poems forthcoming in *Spoor* (Ten Crow Press), *Point Rider's Plain Anthology, Nimrod,* and *Baraza.* Her work has appeared in *Yakima, Calyx,* and *Artsphere.*

FRIDA KAHLO (1920-1954) See page 87. JULIETTA ACKERMAN has a degree in social ecology from the University of California/Irvine. She is fluent in English, Spanish and French. NANCY BRESLOW is writing a book about Frida Kahlo. Her photographs appear in *Salsa y Salero,* a Spanish textbook published by Scott, Foresman, and an article on Kahlo appeared in *Américas.* AMY WEISS NAREA grew up in Mexico City and received her M.A. from Northwestern University. She coordinates a bilingual program for the Chicago Public Schools.

MARIE LUISE KASCHNITZ, born in Karlsruhe, Germany, was raised in Potsdam and Berlin. She was awarded several major literary prizes during the '50s and '60s. After World War II she published poetry and several volumes of *Aufzeichnungen,* or sketches. She died in Rome in 1974. SALLY ROBERTSON graduated from Carleton College with a major in German and has studied in West Germany. She is a member of the American Translators Association. In October she will teach in Austria under the auspices of the Fullbright Commission.

LOUISE LABÉ, a poet of the sixteenth century in Lyon, France, conducted a celebrated literary salon, and is said to have fought at the seige of Perpignan as a soldier in the Dauphin's army. SIBYL JAMES currently works as a freelance editor and writer for magazines and research firms in the Seattle area. Her poems have recently been accepted by *The Little Magazine, The International Poetry Review, Calyx,* and *Tendril.*

LI CHI was educated in her native Chang sha, and in Shanghai, Peking, Nanking, and Oxford. She translated the opening books of Wordsworth's *Prelude* into Chinese verse. She has lived in the United States and Canada for the past thirty years, teaching and translating. Her *Collected Tz'u* and *Shih Poetry* was published in 1975.

GRAÇA MARTINS, born in Vila do Condo, Portugal, participated in the Graphic Arts Design Course at the art school of Portugal. Together with Isabel de Sá she produces *Folheto,* a feminist monthly.

MARGARITA MICHELENA, poet, journalist and magazine editor, was born in Mexico in 1917. Her poetry is widely published. *Renunión de Imágenes,* a volume of her collected poems, came out in 1966. NANCY PROTHRO is a poet-in-the-schools in Montana. She recently completed her Ph.D. studies at the University of Virginia with a dissertation on Wallace Stevens.

RIVKA MIRIAM, an Israeli writer, was awarded the Jerusalem Prize this year for her four published books. Much of her work uses Biblical imagery. LINDA ZISQUIST attended Tufts, Harvard and SUNY at Buffalo. Her poems have appeared in *Niagara Stand* and *Three Rivers Poetry Journal.* A chapbook of translations will be published by Unicorn Press this year. She lives in Jerusalem.

NANCY MOREJÓN has drawn from Cuba's African traditions and her own blackness to offer socially pertinent and feminine poetry. Collections include *Mutismos Y Amor, Ciudad Atribuída,* and *Richard Trajo Su Flauta Y Otros Argumentos,* for which she received an honorable mention by the Union of Cuban Artists and Writers. She is on the staff of *La Gaceta de Cuba.* KAY BOULWARE-MILLER is a lecturer in Latin American literature and Spanish at UCLA with special interest in Antillean literature. She has published in the *Harvard Educational Review, Vórtice Literatura Y Crítica* and *Studies in Afro-Hispanic Literature.*

PETRA VON MORSTEIN was born in Potsdam in 1941 and teaches philosophy at the University of Calgary in Canada. She has published poems and philosophical articles and translated Wittgenstein's *Blue and Brown Notebooks* into German. ROSMARIE WALDROP is editor and publisher of the Burning Deck Press, along with Keith Waldrop. She is author of a translation of Peter Weiss' *Bodies and Shadows,* 1969; *Against Language?,* 1971; and *The Aggressive Ways of the Casual Stranger,* 1978.

THELMA NAVA worked as an editor and founded *Pájaro Cascabel* before returning to poetry. She has since been awarded many prizes and is well recognized in Mexico for her poems. "Almost Summer" is taken from *Colibrí 50.* NANCY PROTHRO, (see Michelena).

ANNA DE NOAILLES (1873-1933) was celebrated in her own time (the *Times,* in 1913, called her the greatest poet of the twentieth century in France and perhaps all Europe) and participated with Proust and Valery in the renewal of French letters. KITTY DELLE ROBBINS teaches French language and literature and has published a number of reviews and essays in literary criticism and women's studies. At present she is working on an essay on archtypes of monster, victim and villainess in contemporary feminist writing.

SUZANNE PARADIS was born in Beaumont, Quebec and graduated from the Ecole Normale in Quebec City. Her collections include *A Temps de Bonheur,* 1960; *La Chasse aux Autres,* 1961; *La Malbête,* 1962; *Pour les Enfants de Morts,* 1964; and *Le Visage Offense,* 1966. She is also the author of *Femme fictive, femme reélle,* 1966. MARYANN DE JULIO teaches French and has recently been a member of the Translation Workshop at the University of Iowa in Iowa City.

HALINA POSWIATOWSKA, poet, writer and translator, was born in 1935. At the time of her tragic death in 1967, she was teaching philosophy at the Jagiellonian University in Cracow, Poland. Her poems convey an intense hunger for life. Books include *Idolotrous Hymn,* 1958; *Today's Day,* 1963; *Ode to Hands,* 1963; and posthumously, in 1968, *One More Recollection.* GRAZYNA DRABIK, poet, translator and sociologist from Poland, presently lives in New York. Her work has appeared, or is scheduled to appear in *Phantasm, Sunbury, Porch, The Chariton Review* and *Ironwood.* She teaches literature in the Slavic department at Columbia University. SHARON OLDS has poems published in *Poetry, The New Yorker, The Atlantic Monthly, The New Republic, The Paris Review,* and *Calyx.* Her first book of poems, *Satan Says,* was published by the University of Pittsburgh Press (Pitt Poetry Series) in 1980.

MARION SETTEKORN, born in 1948 in Hagen, West-Germany, was educated in Berlin, and in Japan, where she studied Calligraphy and Japanese art and language. She plans to return to Japan in 1981 for two years. She has exhibited widely in joint and solo exhibitions in Berlin, Stuttgart, Cologne, Paris, and Düsseldorf, where she has worked and lived since 1978.

EDITH SÖDERGRAN, born in St. Petersburg, Russia in 1892, and raised in Raivola, Finland, grew up speaking Russian, German, Finnish and Swedish. She was educated in St. Petersburg; at sixteen, she contracted tuberculosis, which led to her death in 1923 at age 31. Her first volume of poetry, *Dikter,* appeared in 1916. Her work inaugurated the modern movement in Swedo-Finnish and Swedish poetry.

CHRISTER L. MOSSBERG, born in Skåne, Sweden, emigrated to America as a boy, but never lost touch with the language and its people. He was educated at American colleges and universities, and at Lund University in Sweden. He teaches at the University of Oregon.

NATASA SOTIROPOULOS, born in Lambia, Greece, came to the U.S. in 1965. In 1973 she received a Heintz scholarship, and earned an MFA degree in painting from Carnegie-Mellon University in 1975. Her paintings have appeared in numerous one-woman exhibitions in the U.S. and international group exhibits. She lives in New York City.

ALFONSINA STORNI was the first woman to actively enter literary life in Argentina. Her poems reveal her conflict, rage and despair. She wrote plays, articles and essays, as well as seven books of poetry before she ended her life in 1928 by walking into the sea at Mar del Plata. ALMITRA DAVID holds an MA in Spanish, and now teaches creative writing through the Women's Center of Cedar Crest College in Allentown, PA. She has had poems in *The Beloit Poetry Journal, Earth's Daughters, Hanging Loose, Chomo-Uri,* and *Plainswoman.* JANICE GEASLER TITIEV, a professor at the University of Windsor in Ontario, Canada, has had articles on Alfonsina Storni published in *Kentucky Romance Quarterly, Letras Femeninas,* and *Plexus.*

EVA STRITTMATTER, born in 1930 in Neuruppin, East Germany, studied German literature in Berlin. She worked for the writers' association of the GDR and has published essays of literary criticism in the leading GDR literary journal, *Neue Deutsche Literatur.* She has published five volumes of poetry and in 1975 received the Heinrich Heine Prize. HANNA MOSQUERA, born in 1926 in Freiburg, left Germany in 1939. She holds a degree in anthropology from City University of New York, and an MA in German from University of Iowa. She translates short stories by East German writers at the International Writing Program of the University of Iowa.

WISLAWA SZYMBORSKA, born in Kormik, Poland, studied Polish literature and sociology at the Jagiellonian University in Cracow, where she has lived since 1945. She is poetry editor of *Literary Life,*

and translates French poetry of the 16th and 17th century. She received the Minister of Culture Award for *Salt* in 1963. GRAZYNA DRABIK and SHARON OLDS. (See Poswiatowska.)

TUN WAN-CHENG (ca. 1778-1850) was separated from her husband by his government duties. Her husband's *tz'u* in response to the one translated here survives. LI CHI (see Li Chi) and MICHAEL PATRICK O'CONNOR has published poems in *Triquarterly, Shenandoah* and *Contemporary Literature in Translation.*

GABRIELE WOHMAN, born in Darmstadt in 1932, is a member of PEN and of the Berlin Academy of Arts. Recipient of the Villa Massimo scholarship for 1967/68, she also won the literary Award of Bremen in 1971. Other works include *Ausflug met der Mutter, Abschied für länger,* and a volume of short stories, *Rural Party.* JANET GLUCKMAN is president and founder of Professional Media Services, an editorial and literary agency. She emigrated from South Africa in 1960 and has traveled widely in the U.S., Europe, Africa and the Caribbean. ELIZABETH RÜTHSCHI HERRMAN, is the author of *German Women Writers,* published posthumously in 1979.

YANG CH'E lived during the Ch'ing Dynasty, probably during the first three quarters of it. Nothing else is known of her. LI CHI (See LI CHI) and MICHAEL PATRICK O'CONNOR (see TUN WAN-CHENG).